Deadlier than the Male
x x x

Deadlier than the Male xxx

SCOTLAND'S MOST WICKED WOMEN

Douglas Skelton

BLACK & WHITE PUBLISHING

First published 2003
by Black & White Publishing Ltd
99 Giles Street, Edinburgh EH6 6BZ

ISBN 1 902927 68 0

All photographs courtesy of the author, except:
Edinburgh Tolbooth, Helen MacDougall,
Maggie Laird, Burke's Execution and Calton Jail
courtesy of Edinburgh Central Library,
the Scottish Maiden courtesy of
National Museums of Scotland/SCRAN,
Duke Street Prison courtesy of
SMG/SCRAN
and Sheila Garvie courtesy of SMG.

Cover design by Freight

Printed and bound by Creative Print & Design

Contents

Introduction

Let's make one thing quite clear from the beginning. Men commit the majority of murders. It is an uncomfortable notion, especially if you are a male, but true nonetheless. But, before the sisterhood gets too cocky – if that's a word that can be used when dealing with women – let's also make it clear that a number of those murders are committed on their behalf, at their instigation or simply to impress them. And that doesn't even begin to take into account the number of Norman Bates-alikes out there whose mothers have something to answer for.

Then there are those females who have had a little more hands-on involvement in matters murderous.

There is no doubt about it. Even though women are more often than not victims, the gentler sex does have a brutal side. Wives can murder husbands, lovers and even children. Daughters can kill parents, siblings and friends. They are capable of homicide — both the premeditated type and ones committed on the spur of the moment. You will find examples of them all in these pages.

My trusty edition of the *Concise Oxford Dictionary* tells me that a wicked person is sinful, iniquitous, vicious and given to immorality. Although most of the women, about whom you're going to read, fit that description perfectly, wickedness is a question of perspective. Queen Joan may have had good reason to do what she did to her husband's murderers and the brutality of her revenge was in keeping with the styles of the day. However, the men who assassinated James I really believed they were doing away with a tyrant, whose wife had supported him throughout his reign. From their perspective, especially while they were undergoing hours of horrific torture, she was wicked.

The same could be said for Mary Stuart. She has cut a romantic figure through the ages but if you were to time-warp back to Edinburgh around 1567 and ask someone in the street what they thought, you would receive a different picture. It was strongly believed she had conspired with the man she would later marry to murder her husband, Lord Darnley. So, to many of her contemporaries, Mary, Queen of Scots was a wicked woman.

Jeannie Donald and Susan Newell both killed young children but the question of why they did so remains unanswered. Jean Waddell killed because she would rather hang than go back to a mental institution. Jean Livingston felt forced to kill her abusive husband. Sheila Garvie may also have seen no other way than homicide to get herself out of what had, allegedly, become a hellish marriage. Christina Gilmour may have turned to poison to extricate herself from a match she had never wanted in the first place. The acts were wicked – the people were not. They were confused – some perhaps deranged – but not evil although, understandably, the relatives of the victims saw it somewhat differently.

Other cases detailed here are more clear cut. Maggie Laird and Helen McDougall – spouses of William Hare and William Burke respectively – were up to their necks in the horrors of Edinburgh in the late 1820s. Jessie King knowingly slaughtered at least three babies in 1888. Katharine Nairn first lured her husband's brother into an affair and then used him to help commit murder. Catherine Stuart helped her husband to poison an uncertain number of men in order to plunder their wallets. These are all, without a shadow of a doubt, wicked women.

However, there is one famous Scottish case you will not find here, although it is mentioned once or twice, and that is the Madeleine Smith story. The case of the well-to-do Glasgow girl who very probably poisoned her French lover because his attentions were becoming inconvenient has been well documented by the likes of William Roughead, the doyen of Scottish true crime writers, and Jack House. Although you cannot go anywhere in Scottish murder lore up until the early part of the twentieth century without finding Roughead's fingerprints all over the paperwork, Jack

House's account of the Smith case cannot be bettered.

So, what follows is a blood-spattered trawl through Scottish criminal history. Here is torture, stabbing, hanging, poisoning, bludgeoning, strangling, smothering and shooting. Gentle it ain't.

Happy reading.

Douglas Skelton

1

DEAD OF WINTER

Queen Joan, 1437

The old woman stood before them, her head covered in a shawl, cold fingers of wind reaching out from the choppy waters of the Forth and tugging at her threadbare clothes. Normally, the king and his beautiful queen would not have given the crone a second glance but her words had stopped them before they boarded the boat to ferry them across the river to the north bank. Those words carried a warning, a dire prophecy of impending doom if they chose to spend Christmas 1436 in the Blackfriars Monastery at St Johnstoun, as Perth was known then. A claw-like hand appeared from beneath the long shawl and a gnarled finger pointed at the king, urging him to turn back, to celebrate the Yuletide elsewhere.

The woman amused James I but he ignored the warning. Such predictions were not unusual in medieval Scotland and, if he paid attention to every presentiment of death, he would never go anywhere. So he proceeded to Blackfriars Monastery as planned. Later, the speywife arrived at the gates of the monastery, as if to see how things turned out.

James should have listened to the woman for things turned out very badly – not only for him but also, thanks to his English queen, for the men who plotted his death. For, after her husband's brutal assassination at the hands of a group of Scottish nobles, this unforgiving and single-minded woman supervised a bloody revenge that is unparalleled in the turbulent history of Scotland.

Joan Beaufort had caught the eye of the young James while he was languishing, albeit comfortably, in prison in England. The second son of King Robert III, James became the heir to the Scottish throne following the death of his eldest brother, David, Duke of Rothesay. It was said that David had been starved to death in Falkland Castle by his uncle, the devious and rapacious Robert, Duke of Albany. The Duke desired the return of the Governorship of Scotland which had been taken from him when Robert succeeded to the throne. Robert III, never a strong ruler, had no desire to see his surviving offspring succumb to the ambition of his ruthless brother so he resolved to send young James to the safety of France. However, an ill wind blew the bonnie boat carrying the lad who was born to be king into the path of an English ship at Flamborough Head and he was taken hostage.

He spent eighteen years in the captivity of two English rulers, Henry IV and his successor Henry V. During his time in the south, his father died, they say, from the shock and grief of hearing about his son's capture. Robert had been a good man – if somewhat weak – and he is best summed up by the epitaph he gave himself, 'Here lies the worst of kings and the most miserable of men'. With the old king dead and the young monarch in the hands of the English, Albany seized the regency of Scotland. He proved a strong ruler – far stronger than his father and brother had ever been – but his talent for intrigue and double-dealing saw him enter uneasy alliances with Scottish nobles who believed the land and people were theirs to do with as they wished. This would prove to be their undoing in years to come.

Albany resolutely refused to pay any ransom for the young king's return and the English constantly used the boy as a threat to keep in check any plans the regent had for incursions south. Travelling in the main with the royal court across England, James was also taken to France in 1420 and again in 1421 in a bid to convince Scots fighting for the French army that they were on the wrong side.

Meanwhile, young James was growing into manhood. He was an active lad but his exposure to the English court and long periods of enforced solitude generated in him a love of poetry. He wrote his own verses, including one dedicated to a young girl he had seen from the window of his prison, either while in the Tower of London or, which is more likely, during a term at Windsor Castle. She was, he wrote,

> The fairest or the freshest young flower
> That ever I saw, me thought, before that hour.

The young girl may well have been Joan Beaufort, daughter of the Earl of Somerset. Her grandfather, John of Gaunt, Duke of Lancaster, was one of the most powerful nobles in England. Henry IV was John of Gaunt's son from his first marriage. However, it was his open liaison with his mistress, Katherine Swynford, which resulted in the Beaufort line and ultimately, after a few swings on the family tree, the establishment of the House of Tudor.

The idea of a match between the two young people appealed to both the English king and Joan's family, who were never slow to recognise an opportunity to amass either power or wealth. With one part of the family – even if it were spawned on the other side of a royal blanket – seated on the English throne and another within grasping distance of the Scottish crown, their influence would be considerable. Henry V, no doubt, saw a way to neutralise those troublesome Caledonians for, with a strong Englishwoman at their king's side, they would be less likely to wage war. Being an English king, he did not as much seek an ally of the Scots but loyal subjects to his authority.

James and Joan were married on 2 February 1423 in the Priory Church, St Mary Overy, now Southwark Cathedral. Soon the young king was released to return to his homeland, on the promise of the payment of a 60,000-merk ransom. The sum, ostensibly to pay for James's board and education during his eighteen years of captivity, was to be paid in six annual instalments. And, just to ensure the Scots coughed up, some twenty-one of their nobles were taken as collateral.

In April, the thirty-year-old king travelled north with his

bride. And he returned to find his country at odds with itself. Albany died in 1420, aged eighty-three, and he was succeeded by his son, Murdoch, who, like James, had spent a considerable time in English hands. Albany had managed to free him in 1415 but had somehow failed to engineer the release of his king. Not that he would have wanted to because he was having far too rich a time ruling in James's stead.

Murdoch, though, proved to be far from a chip off the old block. The Scottish barons – no longer beaten, bullied or bought by Albany's strong tactics – felt free to rampage across the land, robbing, ravaging and raping where they pleased.

James also proved to be nothing like his father. A poet he may have been but he was also athletic and a good man with a sword and bow. After being crowned in Scotland's ancient capital at Scone, he was determined to bring the rebellious barons to heel and would do so with a mixture of his uncle's ruthlessness and his father's love of justice. His queen, the fierce blood of the House of Lancaster flowing through her veins, supported him at every turn and she even managed to feather her own nest along the way. Of course, James was a Stewart and the royal purse was ever much on his mind, so a great many of the moves against the nobles were carried out with an eye on boosting his own treasury. Lack of funds, or the pursuit of them, dogged the Stewarts throughout their dynasty and, indeed, one of the men who would wield a dagger against the king was someone to whom James owed money.

First on James's house-cleansing list was his cousin, Murdoch of Albany, the erstwhile regent who was made to regret the payment of the ransom. He and his two sons were charged with treason and promptly beheaded on Gower Hill at Stirling. Then it was the turn of the nobles who were to learn that they were no longer a law unto themselves. In 1428, while holding court in Inverness, James had forty rebellious Highland chiefs brought before him and thrown into the dungeons to await execution. In the end, only three were hanged but the message was received and understood

– here was a king who was not to be trifled with. Their wild and thieving ways would be tolerated no longer. They would toe the line or dangle at the end of it.

He made one incursion against England, besieging the Border town of Jedburgh, which had long been in the hands of the southern invaders. However, the war was cut short by word from his queen in Edinburgh that there were nobles plotting against him. He returned north, much to the disgust of many of his own generals who thought their honour besmirched by turning tail in the face of the jeering English.

Influenced by his time in England, James set about reforming Scots law and democracy, increasing the commoners' rights to justice and even instituting a rudimentary form of legal aid. His sense of justice, though, did not extend to those who preached the reformation of the church. During his reign, the Scottish authorities burned its second heretic at the stake. Their victim was Paul Crawar, a doctor who preached free love and an early form of socialism. He was put to the flame in the market place at St Andrews in 1432, a brass ball bound into his mouth to prevent him from preaching any more of his dangerous notions. An X in the cobbles marks the spot of the conflagration.

How much of this strength of will came from James's love for his wife can only be a matter of conjecture. Certainly, her family possessed more than their fair share of grit and determination. Her grandfather, John of Gaunt, had been High Steward and had shown tremendous – and murderous – abilities in taking on those who opposed the king. To James, his beloved Joan was a 'milk-white dove' but this dove had sharp claws and that could only have helped bolster his campaign to pacify the restless nobles. In the end, though, it was some of those restless nobles who would bring James's rule to a close at that fateful Christmas court.

Prime mover in that regicide was Walter Stewart, the Earl of Atholl and the king's uncle. As the offspring of Robert II, the earl believed himself the rightful king and, at seventy-five years of age, his time was running out fast. His son, Sir Robert Stewart, the king's Chamberlain, was also deeply involved – his eye fixed firmly on the throne that would fall to him when his aged father shuffled off his mortal coil. These men, however, would keep in the background.

The principal player in the bloody acts that were to follow would be their cousin, Sir Robert Graham. He had been arrested during the purge of the Albany boys and their supporters in 1425 but he was later set free. Graham held family enmity for the king and had long been a vociferous critic of his policies. At a meeting of the Three Estaites, he publicly denounced James and, striding across the floor, actually seized the royal person and demanded that he be arrested as traitor. However, on looking around the chamber, Graham realised that he was very much on his own in this endeavour and stormed out. Surprisingly, James let him go but he did take the opportunity to seize Graham's lands while he was off skulking in the Highlands. Later, a price was put on the rebel's head when it was learned that treasonous talk still tumbled from his mouth. Graham subsequently took refuge with one of his kinsman, none other than the Earl of Atholl. He had – surprisingly enough, given his own desire for the crown – been one of the nobles present and unmoving when Graham had tried to depose the king. With all of this ambition and hatred welling up in the breasts of Scots nobles, it was only a matter of time before blood would be spilled.

James and his queen had been at Blackfriars Monastery since Christmas and, on 20 February 1437, they passed a very pleasant day there. They knew the place well for it was the custom of the ruling royals to use it as their residence during visits to the area. Joan had founded the monastery's Charterhouse in 1429. The General Council had sat in the town many times and it was believed that James would have made Perth the nation's capital had an assassin's blade not got to him first.

The day had been spent relaxing and playing chess and other games, listening to music and verse and generally having a good time. As night fell, the king was chatting with his queen who was in her bedchamber, along with her ladies-in-waiting. Meanwhile, Sir Robert Stewart, the Chamberlain, was sealing his treachery by personally opening the doors to the monastery to let Graham and seven heavily armed knights in.

The first casualty that night was the king's page, Walter Straiton, who was slain on the stairs leading to the queen's bedchamber. The murder alerted the king to the situation. Hearing the sound of the men nearing the chamber, he knew there was trouble. Seizing a pair of tongs from the fireplace, he quickly pulled up the planking on the floor and dropped into a vault below. As Queen Joan and some of the ladies-in-waiting swiftly placed the wood back again, the assassination party arrived at the door. One lady went to bar the door against them but the Chamberlain had foreseen this happening and had had the bolts removed. According to legend, Lady Katherine Douglas thrust her arms into the brackets to hold the men off but they soon broke the wood and her arm. Although the story is little more than a legend, this brave act gave her the name Kate Barlass.

What is true is that Queen Joan tried to face down the gang and was wounded in the process. Clearly the murder party was not just here for the king – they wanted the queen too. This would seem understandable for she was also a threat to their ambition – as was her six-year-old child. A blade was laid at her breast but, before the deed could be done, it was knocked away by Sir Thomas Graham – Robert Graham's son. He was having none of the slaying of women and he said so. In this way, the queen was allowed to live although the assassins themselves would live to regret it.

Meanwhile, the loose floorboards were discovered and the men dropped through in pursuit of the king, who had planned to escape through a culvert into the courtyard. However, at his own request, that opening had been blocked off the day before to prevent his tennis balls from bouncing into the basement vault. He was trapped in the chamber. His only option was to fight.

He had come to Scotland a fit and well-built man of thirty but now he was forty-three and, in the words of one early account of the assassination, 'oppressed by his excessive corpulence'. Portly he may have been but, when the first two knights attacked him with knives, the king managed to throw them to the floor but he was badly wounded in the process. Sir Robert Graham came at him next, sword raised. The severely weakened king knew there was little hope for him and asked that he be allowed a confessor. But Sir Robert Graham knew a play for time when he heard it and replied, 'Nae confessor shalt thou hae but this sword.' And then he struck the first blow through the king's chest. His accomplices joined in and together rained twenty-eight strokes on the king's body. They left the mutilated corpse where it lay on the cold stone floor of the vault.

As they made their escape, they were chased by one of the king's men. Before this loyal noble was himself incapacitated, one of the assassins was killed and another was wounded

Back in her chamber, the queen grieved and ignored her own wounds. It would have been better for the killers if they had finished her off, she vowed. For she was now no longer the king's milk-white dove. The fairest and freshest flower was about to show her thorns.

James may have been unpopular with his nobles but the ordinary people loved him – partly *because* he was unpopular with his nobles. As soon as word got out that he had been foully done to death in that cold stone chamber, the cry for vengeance rose in the throats of peasants across the land. Sir Robert Graham and his cohorts may have thought they had made a clean getaway but they found there was nowhere to run and nowhere to hide from the eyes of Queen Joan and her loyal subjects. Within the month the main actors in the conspiracy had been rounded up to face the terrible wrath of the grieving and wounded queen.

The Fourth Chief of the Clan Donnachaidh, Robert of Struan, captured Sir Robert Graham. He brought the assassin to Edinburgh in chains where he was handed into the keeping of Joan and her torturers. Struan – who provided the patronymic for the Robertson family who held lands near Kinloch Rannoch in Perthshire – was made a baron for his service and allowed the right to display a chained man on his coat of arms, as well as a hand supporting the Crown.

All of this mattered little to Sir Robert Graham. The queen ordered a gallows to be set up at Edinburgh's Market Cross. The right hand that had raised the sword against his king was nailed to the gallows' wood and, thus pinned, he was forced to endure a most fearful punishment. Metal spikes were heated over a flame and then forced into various parts of his body. His tormentors were highly skilled in their art for he was not allowed to die until they had cut him to pieces.

Sir Robert Stewart, was infinitely luckier for he was merely hanged and quartered. His father, though, was not so fortunate. Queen Joan and her advisers had devised a very special death for him – one that placed this particular bout of executions at the top of a roll-call of horror.

The Earl of Atholl was publicly tortured over three days. On the first he was brought from the castle gaol to the Market Cross and there he was bound naked to a huge pulley which dragged him into the air by the feet. As the queen watched, the ropes were loosened and his body plummeted, only to be brought up short when the ropes were tightened again. The bone-jarring shock of this early bungee dislocated his limbs. But they were not yet finished with him this day, for he was dragged – screaming in agony no doubt – to a pillory where, on the orders of the queen, he was finally crowned. However, it was not the sort of crown for which he had hungered. This one was red hot metal and bore the legend 'King of Traitors'. Then, and only then, was he taken back to his jail to whimper through the night.

On the second day, it was the turn of the people of Edinburgh to torture the man who had plotted the death of their beloved king. He was dragged through the streets, his joints still dislocated and the crown still on his head. No doubt a few choice words and a variety of missiles were thrown his way.

The third day brought about the end of the Earl of Atholl. He was placed on a plank and, as the Edinburgh mob watched and jeered, he was disembowelled, his organs cut from his body and his private parts hacked off and burned. His head was struck from what was left of the body, held up for the crowd to see and then spiked even higher so the rest of the city could see it as well. His body was quartered and each part sent to other towns for the population to understand what fate lay in store for traitors and regicides. (It should be noted that some say only a paper crown was placed on his head on the first day, with the metal crown being mounted after his head was lopped off and spiked.)

Vengeance having been served, the queen and her son, James, now adapted to life without a husband and father. No sooner had the final blow been struck against the dead king's body than the nobles began to jostle for position. The queen, while personally directing the bloody acts of vengeance, was also looking to her own position. She had escaped death only by a whisker and, if history had taught her anything, it was that life was cheap when men began to lust for a throne. They would not balk at killing her – or her young son. James II was crowned within five weeks of his father's death – this time at Holyrood. He was safe for now in Edinburgh Castle. Archibald, the powerful Earl of Douglas, was made co-regent, along with the queen mother, but he was not a strong man. The nobles, who had been held in check while James I was alive, now began to reive and rob and rally against one another. Rule of the country, meanwhile, was left to whoever had care of the young king. The regent rode out the storm for two years before finally dying in June 1439.

During this time, the young king and his mother were in the care of Sir William Crichton, the keeper of Edinburgh Castle. But Sir Alexander Livingston of Callendar, who controlled Stirling Castle through his son, saw a way to further his own power and contrived to have the boy king brought to his stronghold. Queen Joan may have been part of this plan for it is said that she concealed the young lad in a trunk. Whatever happened, it seems she regretted her decision soon after arriving at Stirling and once again set off back east to Edinburgh, with Livingston and his men not far behind.

Queen Joan decided that she must do something to protect herself and her son in these dangerous and stormy days so, in the summer of 1439, she took herself a husband – Sir James Stewart, known as the Black Knight of Lorn. Her new husband's allegiance lay with the feared Black Douglas family and its leader, the young but dashing William, Sixth Earl of Douglas, who was fiercely loyal to the boy king. However, Livingston was unfazed by this. He forged an alliance with Sir William Crichton and lured the Black Douglas's young leader, William, to a royal banquet in Edinburgh Castle. Earl Douglas had no reason to be suspicious, for his young friend, James II, was to be present.

According to legend, a black bull's head was brought in to the dinner and this was the signal for William Douglas, his brother David and their friend, Sir Malcolm Fleming of Cumbernauld, to be taken, charged with treason and beheaded on Castle Hill. The young king, used once again as a pawn, watched and wept. He had never forgotten the nights of terror that had filled his childhood – the kidnappings and the brutal treachery he had been forced to witness.

However, he had also inherited his mother's undoubted courage and single-minded ruthlessness. When he was of an age to take his own throne, James of the Fiery Face – so named for a livid facial birthmark – proved he also had fire in his belly. He wreaked terrible revenge on the Livingstons and others, proving to be as decisive and politically astute as his father.

But all that came later, after his mother's death on 15 July 1445 at Dunbar Castle. She was still seeking to further her own power and was, at the time, besieged by those who would prevent it. She was buried alongside her beloved first husband at the Charterhouse of Perth she had founded. However, the heady mixture of her strength and the Stewart thirst for power would materialise once again over one hundred years later. Murder and overwhelming ambition would combine in one of the most violent stories in Scottish history.

And at its heart was another beautiful woman.

2

KILLER QUEEN

Mary, Queen of Scots, 1566-7

She could still hear his screams echoing through the hallways and rooms of the sprawling palace.

It had only been a matter of minutes since the group of men had so rudely interrupted her private supper to drag him from her presence. There had been little she could do but protest while a pistol was held at her belly, threatening both her and her unborn child. Now she stood in the small room powerless to help as her friend and confidant was brutally slaughtered.

Screaming, he was. Pleading for mercy. Screeching her name. She could hear the muffled oaths of the armed men as they pursued him through the chambers and, if she listened intently enough, she could perhaps hear the sound of the blades as they were thrust into his flesh time and time again.

Finally all was silent. She spoke no words to the drunken husband at her side because there was nothing she could say to the man who had brought such a bloodbath before her. They stood in the small anteroom and felt what love there had ever been between them die with each dagger stroke.

Then the curtain twitched and one of her ladies returned, ashen-faced and wet-cheeked.

'They have killed him,' she said, her voice breaking. 'They have killed Davie.'

The Queen of Scots sank into a chair and asked, 'Is it so?' Her head sank as she mourned the little man she had come to trust so implicitly – and, in so doing, had made him a target for the ambitions of men. Then she wiped away the salty tears and straightened up in her chair, her face a stiff mask to conceal her rage and terror. She was a queen, after all, and she would behave like one – even if the lisping boy she had married could not behave like a king.

'No more tears,' she told her lady. 'I will study revenge.'

The question that echoes through the centuries is just what form that revenge took. Was that queen instrumental in the murder of her weak and foppish husband? Or was she herself the victim of a male conspiracy?

Mary Stewart became Queen of Scots at the tender age of six days, following the death of her father James V. Old before his time, the thirty-one-year-old king succumbed, it is said, to a heart that had been broken by his army's defeat at Solway Moss in 1542. He had been wounded during the ill-fated campaign against England's king, Henry VIII, and demoralised by the failure of his own barons to support him. He had returned to Linlithgow, where his French wife, Mary of Guise, was in labour, before proceeding to Falkland Palace in Fife.

On 8 December 1542, the child was born – a girl. On hearing the news, James is said to have remarked, 'It cam wi' a lass and it will gang wi' a lass.' The Stewart dynasty was founded when Marjorie Bruce, daughter of King Robert the Bruce, married Walter the Steward and gave birth to the boy who would later become Robert II. Perhaps James felt his baby daughter would not survive long, that she would die in infancy, as his previous two sons had done, and so bring the Stewart line to an end. But the dynasty would continue to flourish until the eighteenth century. However, the last Stewart monarch was, indeed, to be a woman – Queen Anne.

When James V died, Scotland was, once again, a prize to be fought over by ambitious nobles who, if they could not have the actual throne, could at least have the regency. In one corner stood the Earl of Arran, who favoured closer ties with the hated English and who embraced the new Protestant religion. In the other was the Archbishop of St Andrews, David Beaton, a staunch defender of Scotland's ancient alliance with France and an adherent to the Church of Rome. In the middle were the infant queen and her strong-willed French mother.

Henry VIII, naturally, favoured Arran for the position and freed nobles who had been captured at Solway Moss in order that they could return to Scotland to offer their support. In the grand tradition of Scottish nobility, they were paid handsomely for their loyalty. Henry, being a canny political mover, also saw a way of bringing Scotland completely under his corpulent thumb. If a marriage could be brokered between the child queen and his own son Edward, then England would, at last, have complete sovereignty over its troublesome northern neighbour. He thought it would be a terrific idea if the infant Mary were placed in his care until she was of an age to wed. He did not want to rush things, so her tenth birthday would be time enough.

The queen mother was none too keen on handing her daughter over to the monster who had broken with her beloved Church and plundered its riches. She believed Scotland – and her child – would be better served with a marriage to Francis, the French Dauphin.

Arran, meanwhile, thought a match between young Mary and his own son would be more suitable although he did not tell Henry this. Instead, he held back from agreeing a formal treaty until the Tudor king, who was as well known for his patience as he was for his monogamy, decided that more direct action was needed. His idea was that, if the Scots would not give up the lass willingly, then he would rape, burn and pillage her out of the accursed country. During the campaign that became known as the Rough Wooing, Edinburgh was attacked, Jedburgh was put to the flame and Border towns felt the full weight of Henry's ire until the English were given a bloody nose at Ancrum Moor. But they would be back. They always came back.

At the age of nine months, Mary had perched on her mother's knee to be crowned queen at Stirling Castle, completely unaware of the storm raging around her. By the time she was five, the

English did return – the blood that had seeped into the moorland around Ancrum was only a temporary setback. As the army forced its way northwards, defeating the Scots at Pinkie Cleugh near Musselburgh, fears grew for the little girl's safety. She was first moved to Inchmaholme Priory on the Lake of Menteith, to the west of Stirling, and then to Dumbarton Castle. From there, she was to set sail for a new life in France. It was 7 August 1548 and she would not return for another thirteen years. By that time, she would already be a widow and she would be able to speak French better than she could speak either Scots or English. She would also have changed the spelling of her surname from Stewart to the more Franco-friendly Stuart.

The turbulence of Scottish history continued to bump and grind in her absence. Henry VIII ranted and raved south of the Border but brought his ferocious courtship to a halt in 1549. A French army, dispatched to help the beleaguered Scots, supported the interests of the Roman Church against the growing influence of the religious reformers. In 1546, the fat and cruel David Beaton was murdered in his rooms at St Andrew's Castle by supporters of the new faith, his bloated body draped over the walls like a flag. Mary of Guise, now regent, moved against them and laid siege to the castle. The Protestants – joined by the fiery former priest John Knox – held out for a year but the promised reinforcements never arrived from England. But French ships did arrive and they blasted the Scots out of the castle. Knox found himself stretching and straining under the lash on the French penal galley *Notre Dame*. He remained at his oar for around eighteen months then took up residence in England. He then fled, however, when Mary Tudor – Bloody Mary – succeeded to the throne following the death of her sickly brother, Edward.

Mary Tudor was a staunch Roman Catholic and she visited terror on the followers of the new faith as fervently as they had on her fellow believers. Knox preferred the fire to be in his oratory and not licking at his flesh so he took himself off to Geneva. But, by 1559, he was back in his own country, stirring up trouble for

Mary of Guise's cardinals and archbishops until he was eventually accused of heresy. However, many powerful families had cast off the trappings of Rome. They were embracing the new faith, no doubt with an eye on the rich pickings they might get their hands on should the Catholic Church ever be abolished in Scotland as it had been in Henry's England. Knox, with his new friends, staved off the charge. Nobles rushed to be named the Lords of the Congregation, dedicated to upholding the Word of God as approved by the reformers.

Following a riot in Perth sparked by a typically rambunctious sermon by Knox, the queen mother, spurred on by her French relatives and allies, moved against the Presbyterians. Again Scottish nobles felt their interests were better served in siding with Knox and his Lords of the Congregation. Mary of Guise found herself retreating, ultimately finding refuge in Dunbar Castle – where her daughter would more than once seek protection during her dark days. On the arrival of French reinforcements, the queen mother was able to reach out and smite the rebels a terrible blow. The Lords appealed to England and the young Queen Elizabeth who had succeeded to the throne on the death of her half-sister Mary. An army was duly dispatched north and besieged the French force in newly fortified Leith. However, the Scots were none too happy with the idea of fighting side by side with the English so they held back. The result was that most of the casualties were from south of the Border. But Mary of Guise could take no comfort from this – she was in Edinburgh Castle dying of dropsy, a complaint in which fluid gathers in body tissues and cavities, causing agonising swellings. On 11 June 1560, she succumbed to the painful condition – much to the delight of John Knox, who declared it was 'God's judgment'. Her death took the strength out of the conflict and the English and French reached an agreement to withdraw from Scotland.

The Lords of the Congregation formally cut off all contact with the Pope and declared Scotland a Protestant country. However, there was no wholesale plundering of the old church's lands and riches – much to the disappointment of those nobles who had been eyeing them greedily.

It was to this atmosphere of religious ferment and seething rebellion that Mary returned in August 1561. Ironically, she landed at Leith where French and English blood had been spilled so copiously in the name of Scotland. She was eighteen years of age now, a slender, pale-skinned, red-haired beauty, dressed in widow's black, for her husband, the French King Francis, had died just a few months earlier of a brain tumour. It is hoped, for the sake of her vanity, that black suited her because she would seldom be out of it during the next six years.

John Knox never liked his queen, which is not surprising because he was, like many of his contemporaries, a bigoted old hypocrite who gave misogynists a bad name. He had already published his *First Blast of the Trumpet Against the Monstrous Regiment of Women*, a tract attacking the rule of women, specifically the two Marys – Tudor and Guise. It was his belief that a woman at the helm of the ship of state was an abomination before God. Naturally, his views endeared him to neither Queen Elizabeth, nor the third Mary, now home from France. The fact that she was a woman was bad enough for the rabid old rabble-rouser but to have the audacity to be both female and Roman Catholic had him apoplectic with religious rage.

The two had at least four face-to-face meetings over the next few years during which Knox foamed and spat sanctimony like it was going out of style. For her part, Mary listened to his ravings, parried his arguments in her soft French accent and tried to assure her Protestant subjects that she would not be launching a murderous attack on the reformed Church as her cousin, Mary, had done in England. She had already discussed the matter with her half-brother, Lord James Stewart, who had been acting as regent following her mother's death. He had wanted her to embrace the new religion publicly while following the old one in private but Mary's principles would not allow this. She had no desire to kiss her mass goodbye but she did agree not rub her beliefs in the faces of her people. This was not enough for Knox who upbraided her for celebrating mass and for the sin of dancing, which was seen as the work of the devil by the solemn Presbyterians.

The ordinary people warmly welcomed her but many of her lords were less than rapturous, still fearing that she would wish the power of her Church re-established. However, she had other plans. Scotland, Mary hoped, would merely be a stepping stone to a greater power for she believed that she, and not Elizabeth, was the rightful ruler of England. It was this desire to have herself, or her heirs, holding court in the palaces of Westminster that guided her during her brief time in Scotland.

Mary's claim to the throne of England stemmed from the controversy over Elizabeth's birth. As the daughter of Anne Boleyn, the English queen was viewed as illegitimate because Henry had, in the eyes of the Roman Catholic Church, bigamously married the lady of the thousand days. This view was held on account of the Pope's refusal to sanction either his divorce from Catherine of Aragon or the annulment of their marriage. Therefore, on the death of Bloody Mary, Roman Catholics believed that the crown of England should fall to Mary Stuart, through her descent from Margaret Tudor, daughter of Henry VII of England and wife of James IV of Scotland. Elizabeth's claim to the throne was never recognised by the Pope or his loyal followers and Mary was even declared queen of England by her father-in-law Henry II of France. One of the provisos of the 1560 Treaty of Edinburgh, which ended the hostilities between England and France on Scottish soil, was that Mary renounce any claim she had on the English throne. However, Mary point blank refused to ratify the treaty and continued to claim she was England's true queen. This might have seemed like a good idea at the time, given the Stuart (or Stewart) lust for power and wealth, but it would prove to be the death of the Scottish monarch.

Another fatal flaw in her personality, at least according to her many biographers, was her tendency to let her heart rule her head when it came to men although, in some cases, this is a charitable way of looking at her actions. Her romantic decisions, her first marriage apart, can be seen as being totally self-serving and even cynically manipulative.

The subject of marriage was uppermost in the minds of the men who surrounded her at the Scottish court. Uninvited the queen may have been but, now that she was here, they must turn their minds to finding her a husband. She was reckoned to be a fine-looking woman and her beauty had inflamed the hearts and groins of many a man. Even old John Knox – who, despite his outspoken views, had quite an eye for the ladies – commented on her beauty between torrents of religious abuse. He may have seen her as the Whore of Babylon but she was quite a fetching one. One French admirer, the poet Pierre de Chatelard, became too ardent in his attentions and hid himself in her Holyrood bedchamber with a view to taking his love on to a more physical plane. He was caught before he could unfasten his doublet and he was banished from Scotland. However, he followed the queen on one of her many tours of the realm – or royal progresses – and, while she was visiting Rossend Castle in Burntisland, he once more forced his way into her room and tried to rape her. Again he was caught and, this time, he was carted off in chains to St Andrews where, on 22 February 1563, he was beheaded in the town market place. Mary watched the proceedings although her half-brother, James Stewart, now Earl of Moray, may have forced her into this.

De Chatelard was not the only young man with such an interest in the queen but it was vital that she be married off to someone of influence. Among the matches mooted were Don Carlos, son of the King of Spain, and Charles, Archduke of Austria. Mary's French in-laws met neither suggestion with much enthusiasm.

Elizabeth of England, meanwhile, put forward her former lover Robert Dudley, Earl of Leicester. He was, however, suspected of having murdered his first wife by assisting her in a fall down some stairs. Elizabeth hinted that, if Mary would consider marrying an Englishman, then she would, in turn, consider naming her as heir to the throne. Mary, though, was suspicious of Elizabeth's motives, as well she might have been, and, in any case, she did not want any of the so-called Virgin Queen's cast-offs. What she did not know was that good Queen Bess had a fall-back position.

In February 1564, at Wemyss Castle on the Fife coast during one of her many progresses, Mary met Henry Stuart, Lord Darnley. He was the son of the Earl of Lennox, who had been banished from Scotland for having ill-advisedly sided with the English during one of the many disagreements between the two countries. His lands had been declared forfeit to the Crown and he had settled in England, where Henry and his brother, Charles, were born. Henry was educated in France, he had adopted the French spelling of his surname and, by the time he met Mary, he was a good-looking, if slightly effeminate, eighteen-year-old. Surrounded as she was by older men, Mary would have noticed him immediately. Later she described him as the 'lustiest and best proportionat lang man' she had ever seen.

He came to Scotland with his father who had returned to petition for the return of family lands. Darnley had other ideas though – he fancied himself king. He was of royal blood himself – his grandmother had been the sister of Henry VIII – and so he had a strong claim to the throne of England. Mary would have known this, of course, and the thought of taking yet another step closer to the English crown may well have influenced her affections towards him. Whatever the case, a relationship developed. This did not please the Earl of Moray as he had disliked Darnley from the start. The young man, though handsome, was a spoilt brat with a tendency to throw childish tantrums whenever he failed to get his own way. Moray's views, of course, could have been influenced by the thought of losing power over the queen.

Elizabeth was also displaying some opposition to the match. Darnley was a Roman Catholic and such a marriage was not necessarily good news for Protestant England. But Elizabeth, the cunning vixen, was playing a double bluff. She knew that Mary would be attracted to the charming, if vain, young man and she also knew that, by pulling against the match, Mary was likely to pull the other way. Elizabeth also believed that, although Darnley was a Catholic, he was sympathetic to the Protestant cause and having him in a position of authority in Scotland would, in fact, be excellent news for England. So, just to give the Scottish queen a nudge in the right direction, Elizabeth issued an ultimatum regarding the Dudley suit. The ploy worked for, despite advice to the contrary from her half-brother and other nobles – or perhaps even because of it – Mary finally announced she was going to marry Darnley. She appeared to be unaware that she had, perhaps, been manoeuvred into the decision by her more politically astute cousin in the south, who was counting on Mary's unfailing Stuart ambition.

Things had not exactly been easy for Mary up until now. But they were about to become a great deal worse.

While Darnley was courting Mary, he became friendly with a hunchbacked little Italian musician who had managed, through his ingratiating manner and enjoyable company, to worm his way into Mary's confidence.

Much has been suggested about David Rizzio or Riccio. It is claimed he was a papal spy, which was probably not true, but he was a foreigner and a Catholic and, as such, far too close to Mary for the comfort of many Scots barons. His rise through the ranks of the queen's staff was swift and, eventually, he became her personal secretary. Soon he was insisting that any business with the queen should be cleared with him first. And a little bribery was always welcome.

Moray had already fallen out of favour with his half-sister, Mary, thanks to his opposition to the royal marriage. Had his criticisms remained verbal then he could perhaps have ridden out the storm. However, he, along with other Lords of the Congregation, had the audacity to raise a standard against her and Mary personally led a small army to pursue them across the country. There were no real hostilities during this rebellion, merely a catch-me-if-you-can gallop across moss and heather that became known as the 'Chaseabout Raid'. Moray and his Presbyterian lords eventually found sanctuary in England and Mary returned to Edinburgh, her legend further strengthened by the fact that she had donned armour and pistol to protect her throne. What was not so well known, though, was that she had secretly arranged to get assistance from Catholic Spain if she needed it and that she had vowed to protect the Roman Church in Scotland as part of the price for permission to marry from the Pope.

When Mary fell pregnant, she began to neglect matters of state and left many of them to her grasping little secretary. This irritated not only the remaining nobles but also Darnley, who saw the power that he had lusted after was now in Rizzio's hands. He had married Mary but had not been declared king. That prompted a momentous sulk so, when wagging tongues suggested that his wife was cuckolding him with the upstart Italian musician, he was more than ready to believe it. He even began to believe that the child Mary was carrying was not his.

A movement towards granting him the Crown Matrimonial, and so making him king of Scotland, gathered impetus, backed by Moray in exile in Newcastle. A number of their lordships still in Scotland put their names to a document backing the plan. Only James Hepburn, Earl of Bothwell, and John Gordon, Earl of Huntly, remained loyal to the queen. All that was needed to seal the document was blood. And Darnley's old friend David Rizzio was selected to provide it.

On a dark and wet evening in March 1566, the six-months pregnant Mary was enjoying a private supper in an anteroom off her chambers on the second floor of Holyrood Palace. Bothwell and Huntly had been decoyed elsewhere and Moray was, at that time, en route from Newcastle with a company of soldiers.

It was – and is – a tiny space and must have been particularly cramped that night, for dining with Her Majesty were her half-sister the Countess of Argyll, another half-brother, Lord Robert

Stewart, Commendator of Holyrood, and a few other friends, including David Rizzio. The first sign of impending trouble came in the shape of Darnley, who appeared through the tapestry that hid a private staircase leading to his own rooms directly below the queen's. He was filled with good humour and copious amounts of wine. His high spirits alone, considering his recent petulance, were enough to create suspicion.

Then the others began to arrive. First came Lord Ruthven, his body armoured, his face sallow and drawn through illness. But he was well enough to point to the queen's secretary at the far end of the table and say, 'May it please Your Majesty to let yon man Davie come forth of your presence, for he has been ower long here.'

It did not please Her Majesty to let Davie go anywhere and certainly not with an armed and armoured man. She asked what offence Rizzio had given and the red-eyed Ruthven replied, 'Great offence.'

Mary ordered Ruthven to leave but he refused. She stood up and was grabbed by Darnley. Rizzio, smelling death in the air, drew his dagger and stepped behind his friend and queen. Ruthven made a grab for him but, when blocked by Mary's companions, he turned and spat angrily, 'Lay no haunds on me for I'll no be handlit.'

And then the others, including Lord George Douglas, Darnley's uncle, arrived. If space was limited before their arrival, it was now a veritable crowd scene. There was a struggle, during which every candle but one was knocked over as Rizzio tried to evade the assassins. Lady Argyll grabbed the only remaining candle and the grisly scene that followed was played out in the flickering of the solo flame. Shadows danced across the walls as the various voices merged in a cantata of death – Rizzio screaming, the gruff nobles rasping oaths, the queen calling for order.

Mary tried to save her friend but one of the men pointed a pistol at her belly making her fear she was also a target. Rizzio tried once again to shield himself behind her but his fingers were prised away from her skirts and he was dragged away, struggling and screaming for help. But no one helped. No one could. Mary ordered the men to stop but they were on a mission. Also, they had the permission of her husband, who stood behind his wife, his face flushed red from the wine and the excitement. As Rizzio was carried from the small room, Ruthven told Darnley to comfort his wife and assure her they meant her no harm. They must have known that such trauma could well have brought on a miscarriage, which would have played into Darnley's hands, considering he had chosen to believe the child was not his. And, should Mary die in the process, then he would, naturally, finally become king.

David Rizzio suffered a horrific death. He dragged himself across the hallway, still trying to avoid the fate these men had decided for him. He screamed for help in French, appealing to Mary, 'Save my life, Madame, save my life!' But that life was not for the saving. The grim-faced men stalked him as he pulled himself along by his fingertips, lashing out with their daggers again and again, Rizzio's lifeblood dripping to the wooden floor. They stabbed him fifty-six times that night, the final stroke coming from a dagger belonging to Darnley which was left, buried to the hilt, in the already lifeless body. Then he was tossed down the stairs and stripped before finally being tipped into a pauper's grave in Holyrood Cemetery.

Lord Ruthven returned first to the queen and collapsed into a chair, his hands wet with Rizzio's blood. He asked for wine and the queen, having already been told that her secretary was dead, turned her now cold gaze on him and said, 'I trust that God, who beholdeth all things from the high heaven, will avenge my wrongs and move that which shall be born of me to root out you and your treacherous posterity.' Years later, her son James VI did, in fact, root out the Ruthven line and wipe it from existence. But he had reasons of his own for doing so, including revenge for being abducted by the family as a youth and then, later, claiming they had tried to assassinate him.

Meanwhile, the assassins sought out Bothwell and Huntly, as they were considered dangers to their plans, but they had already made their escape. News of the murder and the threat to the queen reached the city of Edinburgh and the provost gathered together a small army of townsfolk to march down the High Street to save her. However, the conspirators had foreseen this and the palace gates were closed against them. The mob demanded news of the queen but only Darnley appeared at a window to reassure them. Meanwhile, a dagger was held at Mary and she was warned she would be 'cut into collops' if she made any sound. However, her husband did not convince the people and he angrily said to them, 'Do you not know I am king? I command you to pass home to your house.' Finally the people's army dispersed.

Mary knew her husband was part of the murder chain but she also recognised him as the weakest link. Within hours of Rizzio's, death she was playing up to him, flattering him, telling him she believed dangerous men had used him and even now were probably plotting against him. Darnley, perhaps shocked at the ferocity of the attack on his former friend, fell for it.

The following day Mary received Moray, apparently unaware that he was a prime mover in the conspiracy. She smiled with him and drank with him and discussed the situation with him. She told the assassins there would be no action taken against them. But all the while she was plotting her escape. Along with Darnley, she stole out of Holyrood Palace in the dead of night and galloped for Seton House near Tranent. After resting there, they headed for Dunbar where Bothwell and Huntly waited with a strong body of supporters.

Mary had played the game and played it well. By managing to bring Darnley over to her side she had put the fear of death into the principal conspirators. His support was vital to their plan and his being back at his wife's side could only mean their lives were forfeit. Then, as news that an 8000-strong army heading their way reached them, discretion was deemed the better part of valour and they fled south. Even John Knox wisely took himself off to Ayr where he continued to rant against the woman he saw as the royal whore. Moray, though, stayed where he was, secure in the knowledge that the queen did not suspect his part in the plot.

With her husband back in the fold, at least for the moment,

Mary declared that Rizzio's murderers must be brought to justice. Two of the murderous band, Tom Scott, Under-Sheriff of Perth, and Henry Yair were caught, tried and beheaded.

The question remains over what Mary thought of Darnley. She knew he was a fickle, weak young man who could change sides as soon as things were not going his way. He was also a womaniser and stories of his infidelities were legion. And then there was her unborn child to consider. Darnley had proved willing to risk a miscarriage both during the Rizzio murder and the subsequent wild ride to Dunbar, when he had parried her objections over the effect it could have on the child in her womb with the statement that, if she miscarried, they could have more. He had been badly frightened then and desperate to get away from the men who had so recently been his co-conspirators. What were his plans for that child now? These are questions she would have pondered as she went into confinement in Edinburgh Castle. She may have reached a somewhat desperate solution.

On 19 June 1566, the Stuart claim to the throne of England was strengthened by the addition of one baby boy, the sixth in the Stuart line to be named James. On hearing the news, Elizabeth made the famous statement, 'The Queen of Scots is lighter of a fair son and I am of but barren stock.' The not so proud father had, once again, taken the huff. He still believed the boy was not his but Rizzio's and even the queen's assurance that the boy had been 'begotten by none but you' failed to put his mind at rest. However, although Mary needed his acceptance of the boy to assure the succession, she may have already formulated other plans for her husband, who was feeling increasingly isolated. The surviving nobles involved in the Rizzio plot felt betrayed by him, while Mary's supporters, principally the Lords Huntly and Bothwell, trusted him a little less than they could throw him.

Bothwell, in particular, was a danger. He was growing closer to the queen than even Rizzio had been. But Bothwell was not as easy a target as the Italian. He was no courtier but a man of action – rough in his manner, quick in his temper and skilful with his sword. When he was wounded during hand-to-hand combat with Border reiver Jock Elliot, Mary rushed from Jedburgh, where she was overseeing a court of justice, to his fortress at Hermitage to consult him on matters of state. The eighty-mile round trip was completed in a single day, which shows how important the Border lord had become to her.

On the return journey she fell into a marsh, became seriously ill and almost died. Years later, with her life and ambitions in ruins, she looked back on the days during which she had hovered on the edge of life in Jedburgh and wished she had succumbed to the fever.

Bothwell, steeped in the Border art of feud, was not a man to let Darnley's actions go unpunished. Mary's Stuart blood would not allow her to forgive her husband's treachery or let a continuing threat to the safety of her royal line go unchecked. Divorce was not an option, thanks to her religion, while an annulment may have cast doubt on the legitimacy of her son's birth. Some other means had to be found to counter the threat posed by the queen's preening puppy of a husband. Whether Darnley knew it or not, he was not long for this earth.

Apologists for Mary say she had no knowledge of the plot supposedly hatched by Bothwell, Huntly and others. Although it is likely that they might have kept certain details from her to provide plausible deniability, it is probable that she knew something was afoot.

Darnley was still smarting over being cold-shouldered in favour of Bothwell but it did not stop him fornicating his merry way through the bawds and harlots of Edinburgh and Stirling. Finally, in 1567, he came down with a pox although the precise nature of the infection is a mystery. The disease ravaged his face and the vain Darnley took himself off to Glasgow's Lennox Castle, which stood on the site now occupied by the city's Royal Infirmary.

Mary arrived in the city to visit her ailing husband, possibly staying in Provand's Lordship, the oldest building in the city. She was there to convince Darnley to return to Edinburgh. She told him there were plots against him and he could be protected better there. Darnley, never the sharpest arrow in the quiver, believed her but, with the brutal slaying of Rizzio still fresh in his mind, did not wish to return to Holyrood. For her part, Mary did not want her infant son open to whatever infection was rampaging through his father's body. Instead, Darnley agreed to take up residence at Kirk O' Field, a house near the city limits, dwarfed by the jagged edge of Salisbury Crags.

It was here that the royal couple were reconciled. Or so it seemed. As Darnley lay in his sick bed, his face covered by a cloth to hide the hideous eruptions, Mary sat by his side, ministering to him, reading to him, relaying court gossip. Finally, on Sunday 9 February, she attended a wedding at Holyrood but did take the time to visit her husband accompanied by Bothwell, Huntly and other nobles. Decked in their finery, the men threw some dice and made pleasant conversation. But the stakes that night were higher than those on the gaming table. Finally, it came time for them to return to the revelries and Darnley, his face still swathed in the cotton mask, complained bitterly about being deserted. Mary assured him she would be back the following day and gave him a ring as a parting gift.

At two the following morning, a huge explosion from near the city walls awakened the city. The house at Kirk O' Field had been demolished after someone had set off a huge store of gunpowder in the basement. Darnley and his valet were dead, their bodies being found a short distance away under a pear tree. Reports suggested they had both been throttled. Perhaps they had been alerted because the gunpowder had been discovered before the fuse was ignited. Perhaps they had tried to get away and been caught in the garden by the assassins. Or, perhaps, by some freak, the explosion had killed them but had left their bodies unmarked and thrown clear of the rubble. The strangulation charge may have then been concocted later.

Bothwell's name was soon in the frame for the murder but there is no firm evidence linking him with the crime, even though the house belonged to the brother of one of Bothwell's friends. Nor is there any firm evidence linking Mary to her husband's death. Darnley had enemies on all sides and it is possible that one, or more, conspired to rid the country of him and his queen. Perhaps the gunpowder stored in the cellar was supposed to go off when the queen and her supporters were together on the night of the wedding.

However, only Mary and Bothwell seemed to benefit from Darnley's death. Mary had removed one potential danger to herself and her son and Bothwell was rid of the man who was married to the woman he desired for himself. That Bothwell had some notions regarding the queen there can be no doubt but whether they were of a romantic or a self-serving nature is less clear. Rumours that the two had been lovers were rife and, although Darnley's death did remove one obstacle to their union, it also threw up another one – but one that Mary, in her customary arrogance, ignored.

After a two-day period of mourning, she and Bothwell left the city and travelled to Seton House where they played golf and organised archery contests. The people, though, were unhappy with the way matters were progressing. Whereas they had formerly taken their young queen to their hearts – with some reservations regarding her religion, certainly – they now turned against her. Knox's accusations over her sexual abandon were being openly repeated in the streets and, in a bid to soothe the affronted morals of the masses, pressure was brought to bear on Mary to instigate some sort of inquiry into Bothwell's alleged complicity in Darnley's murder. Reluctantly, she agreed but, when the time came. Bothwell filled Edinburgh with his own men, no witnesses were called and the swashbuckling Borderer challenged anyone, who thought that he was guilty, to trial by combat. He was, unsurprisingly, acquitted.

Bothwell wanted to marry Mary but he had one problem – he already had a wife. However, she was quite happy to be rid of him, filing for divorce on the grounds of a convenient infidelity with a serving lass. But still Mary hesitated. Despite the ever-growing tide of public opposition, the way now lay open for Mary Stuart and Bothwell to be together. Finally Bothwell, man of action that he was, took matters into his own hands by apparently abducting her at Bridge of Almond near Edinburgh and carrying her off to the stronghold at Dunbar, the castle to which she and Darnley had fled following Rizzio's murder. How willing Mary was in this turn of events is unknown but she did prevent her own protectors from taking any action. At Dunbar the relationship reached a physical level but whether it was rape or consensual depends on your view of the couple in question. In May 1567, Bothwell obtained his divorce and Mary made him Duke of Orkney. She told her council that she wished no action to be taken against him for the abduction. In fact, she was going to marry him.

The news shattered what support she had. To begin with, the ceremony was a Protestant one and that angered her own Church. Her allies in France and Spain were also against the match. Bothwell's enemies wanted to separate the couple and the common people still believed they had conspired to murder Darnley. Finally, while the now married couple were at Borthwick Castle, a force of 1000 men arrived to arrest Bothwell. The canny Borderer managed to escape and left Mary to deal with the posse before she slipped past them disguised as a boy. Reunited with her new husband, they took refuge in the all-but-impregnable Dunbar Castle, with which Mary was by now becoming very familiar.

With her lords forming a confederation and now in open rebellion, Mary and Bothwell raised an army to defend her crown and their marriage. The two forces met at Carberry Hill, near Musselburgh and very close to the site of the battle of Pinkie Cleugh which had led to the child Mary being spirited from the country all those years ago. However, there was to be no blood shed on this occasion. The confederate lords demanded that Mary give Bothwell up to them. Bothwell, as was his habit, challenged anyone, who thought they were hard enough, to single combat but the first challenger to come ahead was dismissed for not being of a lofty enough position to trade blows with the new Duke of Orkney. As the wrangling continued, Mary's army grew bored and began to desert. Finally, Bothwell realised no good was going to come of this continual bickering so he suggested they return to Dunbar. But Mary, who perhaps now saw there was no future with the maverick noble, opted to stay with the confederate lords. Again, it could be argued that the spirit of self-preservation had risen in her breast and she was happy to throw her new lover to the wolves. Or perhaps she felt it advisable that he get away to raise another army. Whatever the case, the lovers were parted on that field and never saw one another again. He went into exile and ended up forgotten, but not gone, in a Norwegian prison, where he eventually succumbed to a gangrenous wound.

If Mary thought she would fare well with the confederate lords, she was sadly mistaken. By giving herself into their hands, she had effectively destroyed everything for which she had worked – and possibly killed – to keep. She was imprisoned and forced to abdicate in favour of her son, the infant James. Her half-brother Moray, proving to be something of a survivor in Scottish politics, was once again named regent. However, his luck ran out in 1570 when he was shot in the stomach as he rode through Linlithgow.

But Mary did not submit willingly to her fall from grace. Despite miscarrying twins, her charms proved useful in luring a young man to aid her in a dramatic escape from imprisonment at Loch Leven Castle. She then led her army of loyal Highland supporters against Moray's force at Langside in Glasgow. The resulting defeat forced a despondent Mary to seek refuge with her cousin, Elizabeth, in England. However, suspicion was strong that, not only was she involved in Darnley's murder, she was also at the centre of various plots to take the place of the English queen. Letters had been found, allegedly written by Mary while she was staying in Glasgow, which proved she was involved in the murder plot. The originals were never actually seen – what was produced were transcripts or copies – but the so-called Casket Letters, named after the silver box in which they were found, were generally accepted at the time as proof of her guilt. She had also never renounced her claim to the

English throne and more letters were supposedly uncovered, during her nineteen years of captivity, that alleged she was at the centre of rebellious plots. Her attitude at her trial – that she could be judged only by God and not by any court of man – failed to go down well in a court filled with men who thought they were somewhere just below God in the pecking order.

Elizabeth was not keen to order the death of her cousin – perhaps because she knew some of the evidence was fabricated. Finally, though, she saw to it that the execution warrant was hidden among other innocent papers so it could be signed as if by mistake. The farcical pretence played out, Mary Stuart was beheaded at Fotheringay on 8 February 1587.

The story of Mary, Queen of Scots, is filled with mysteries. There was so much intrigue but so few records that it is impossible to say with any certainty who was responsible for what. Mary herself cuts a highly romantic figure and, even today, it is easy to dismiss much of what happened as a conspiracy by a male-dominated society. Mary, though, must shoulder much of the blame for the blood spilled during her few years in Scotland. She was arrogant and ambitious. She saw the Scottish crown as third rate compared to those of France and England. She used men just as easily as they were prepared to use her. Despite the change of spelling, she was a Stewart and throughout their history, from their beginnings in Ayrshire to their final days on the throne, the Stewarts put themselves first and everything else second. Nothing was allowed to get in the way of their right to rule – not the people, not the nobles, not religion. Mary often acted solely to protect her own power base and that of her son, who inherited much of his mother's steely determination.

Or did he? For, according to legend, Mary's son died soon after birth and another child was substituted for him. This baby was the newborn second son of the Countess of Mar, in whose care Mary's infant had been placed while Mary went off to plan her husband's downfall. It is said the adult James VI bore little likeness to his father or even to earlier Stewarts but he did bear a strong resemblance to John, the Second Earl of Mar, with whom he shared a particular bond. Was this a family resemblance and a brotherly bond?

It is, of course, only legend. But, in 1830, they say, following a fire in the rooms used by Mary in Edinburgh Castle, a small coffin was found behind a wall. There were bones inside the tiny casket – the bones of a child only one or two months old. And those bones were wrapped in rich silk. And that rich silk was embroidered with a letter, which was either a *J* or an *I – I* being used in Latin for *J*.

Was this the final resting-place of Mary's boy child who had died in infancy? And did a changeling take his place on the throne of Scotland and later England? If so, then James V's prediction that the Stewarts' reign 'cam wi' a lass and will gang wi' a lass' proved correct.

OFF WITH THEIR HEADS

Scottish justice – and its brother-in-law, the Kirk – favoured a number of ways to punish the wicked. Some of them caused little more than embarrassment and discomfort. Others were devised to cause tremendous agony and disfigurement. Death, naturally, was the final solution.

For relatively minor transgressions, men and women could be forced to do penance either by sitting on the 'cutty' or repentance stool or by standing on the pillar or raised platform, in front of the entire congregation. They might also be chained in the 'jougs', manacles set in the wall beside the main church door, or – in the case of nagging, gossiping or slanderous women – be forced to wear the 'branks' or the scold's bridle. This was a metal headpiece with a spiked tongue that was thrust into the mouth to prevent speech.

For more serious offences there was a variety of punishments to hand. Thieves could be branded with the letters *T* or *M* (for Malefactor). In 1701, a Dumfries woman, Elspeth Rule, was burned on the cheek and the branding iron was so hot that smoke blew out from the inside of her mouth. Habitual offenders, such as Anne Harris of Inveraray in the early eighteenth century, often had been branded so frequently that there was very little unmarked flesh on their faces and hands where new letters could be burned. Other punishments, even for comparatively minor offences, included: holes being bored in tongues; hands and ears being lopped off; and the guilty being whipped, tortured, consigned to slavery or banished.

Death sentences could also be dished out for the pettiest of crimes and, again, there was a host of ways to carry them out. Hanging was always a favourite (*see* 'Platform Parties', pp. 141–5). Women could be drowned for theft or witchcraft although the favoured punishment for the latter was burning at the stake. During the witch craze, that began in the reign of Mary, Queen of Scots and peaked while her son was on the throne, an incredible number of women were first 'wirreit' – strangled whilst at the stake – then burned in the name of Christ. But the small mercy of being throttled was a stage that was sometimes dispensed with and the accused 'brunt quick' (burnt alive). Lady Jane Douglas suffered this fate in 1535 after being accused, by her former brother-in-law, of conspiring to murder James V. She was, of course, innocent but that did not stop the authorities from stretching her on the rack to force a confession and then taking her to Edinburgh's Castle Hill, the favoured site for such roastings. There she was tied to a stake, surrounded by barrels of tar and burned.

Some prisoners, usually nobles, preferred being beheaded to being turned off the gallows and slowly throttled on the end of a rope or being strangled and then burned. If they had to go, then beheading was the way. Messy it may have been but it was a much more dignified way to go. For such dispatches, a sword was used, wielded by the common executioner who, like as not, was blind drunk, having received part of his fee in ale. Fairly often the execution was botched, sometimes multiple strokes being necessary to separate the head from the body. Even in a time when barbarity was not just common but was actually a much sought-after form of entertainment, these badly executed events caused distress among the good people of Edinburgh, Glasgow, Aberdeen or Stirling. They did not mind satisfying their morbid curiosity by watching someone die a swift death but they did not want to lose a perfectly good breakfast, thank you very much, by seeing it turn into a bloodbath.

As nothing could be done about the blood, the only thing the authorities could address was the inefficiency of the swordsman.

It was decided that a new way of head-lopping had to be found – something more efficient, more scientific. According to legend, it was James Douglas, Earl of Morton, who brought back the idea of a beheading machine, rather like the one used in the Yorkshire town of Halifax. The Halifax Gibbet was a notorious device which prompted beggars to intone, 'From Hull, Hell and Halifax, the good Lord deliver us.' It stood as a permanent fixture on Gibbet Hill and was a very busy machine indeed for, during the sixteenth century, when it was used, people could be put to death just for stealing a loaf of bread. Exactly when – or even if – the man who later became Regent Morton brought back the idea of such a beheading device is unclear. What is certain, though – and contrary to the popular legend – is that he was not the first to succumb to the Scottish version. That honour fell to Tom Scott, executed for his involvement in Rizzio's murder (*see* p. 35). Jealous rivals, however, implicated Morton in the murders of both David Rizzio and Lord Henry Darnley, and James VI was happy to believe that the man who played regent during his early years was involved in the death of the father he never knew. After a whirlwind trial, with evidence provided by servants tortured into saying what the prosecution wanted, on 2 June 1581 Morton was led to the device he was credited with bringing to Scotland.

Halifax and Scotland were not alone in having beheading machines. Germany and Italy both had their own such devices, as did France, even before Dr Joseph Guillotin came up with his famous design to strike off a man's head 'in the twinkling of the eye, and you never feel it.'

The Scottish machine swiftly became known as 'The Maiden' although exactly why is not known. Some say it was because the word for 'place of execution' in Gaelic was *Mod-dun*, which is as good a theory as any. A replica stands in Edinburgh's Museum of Scotland – a 10-foot-high wooden structure with a 5-foot-wide beam at its foot and another long diagonal beam supporting it. The iron blade is just over 10 ins long and topped with lead weights because the weight of the blade itself is not enough to slice through a neck successfully. The grooves on the facing edges of the uprights were kept well greased to allow the smooth downward passage of the blade.

The beauty of The Maiden was that anyone could use it. Pull the pin and down the blade went. Theoretically, there was no need for a special executioner to turn up with his double-handed sword. Labourers had to be paid to transport the device to the place of execution, for the Scottish version was a portable affair, but then labourers had to be paid to construct a gibbet. A blacksmith also had to be paid to sharpen the blade but that was a small price to pay for such an efficient means of dispatching malefactors.

In 1600, The Maiden was the instrument of death for a young woman of barely twenty, convicted of having her husband murdered. Her family wanted her execution to be performed as quietly as possible but the people were not to be deprived of their spectacle. Meanwhile, her co-accused, two women without the benefit of being high born, were put through the hell of strangling and burning.

3

DEATH AND THE MAIDEN

Lady Jane Warriston and Janet Murdo, 1600

Exactly when Lady Jean Livingston of Dunipace married John Kincaid, Laird of Warriston, is unclear. She was born in 1579, the daughter of a wealthy and influential Stirlingshire family, and died in 1600, so they could not have been wed too long before Kincaid met his brutal end. A popular ballad about the affair had it that they had been married 'these nine years running ten', which does seem unlikely. Another version says she married him at fifteen. Yet another says that the match was made not in heaven but in profit; in other words, she married the considerably older Laird of Warriston for money. However, soon after the wedding, she gave birth to a young son. Whether it was her husband's child is open to some question, however, given her curious relationship with one of her father's servants.

Whatever the case, matrimonial bliss definitely eluded the beautiful young woman. Again the reason for this is shrouded in some mystery. The balladeers insist her husband was an uncaring brute who regularly dished out beatings. According to a later indictment (not against her but a male co-accused), she developed 'ane deadly rancour' against her husband for 'the alleged biting of her on the arm and striking her divers times'.

But ballad-makers were not known for letting the facts get in the way of a good story. Their function was to entertain and it did not suit their yarn if the main character was unsympathetic. So, without the benefit of any decent records regarding the events leading to the actual murder, we have to make do with what could be half-truths or even downright fantasy.

49

So let us just assume that Lady Jean Livingston was incredibly beautiful. Let us also assume that she married the older John Kincaid because her family wished it and, further, that Kincaid was a brute who made her life a misery.

The story goes that, after one nasty experience at the dinner table, the Laird was so unhappy with his young wife's conversation that he threw a dinner plate at her and split her lip. She ran weeping to her bedroom where the devil appeared before her to entice her into the ways of sin. It is highly unlikely that Satan made such an entrance although her nurse, Janet Murdo, may have influenced Jean.

'He's not good enough for you, lamb,' the older woman might have said as she comforted her young charge. 'No woman should have to put up with that treatment,' she might have continued, truthfully. 'Something should be done about him. Something permanent.'

Perhaps the young Lady Warriston resisted the notion at first but might have grown more amenable to the suggestion as her husband's behaviour worsened. Finally, she agreed that her desperate situation called for a desperate remedy and the nurse said, 'I know just the man to help us.'

At that time, Jean's father, Sir John Livingston, was enjoying the good graces of James VI – not exactly a secure position, for Stuart monarchs were notoriously mercurial in their friendships. But, still, he held a position of some influence. As one of the king's loyal advisers, he was in residence at Holyrood. The nurse left Warriston, which at the time was an estate on the outskirts of the city, and walked the mile to the palace below Arthur's Seat to seek out a groom, Robert Weir, who had been in the service of Sir John for a number of years. Bonnie Jean would, no doubt, have known him while she was growing up in the family home at Dunipace. Whether there had been any form of romantic link between the two is unrecorded but this is certainly hinted at in some accounts. Such a forbidden love – she was high born, after all, and he was but a glorified stable lad – would certainly explain why he was willing to turn killer on her behalf. However, even though his name was at the top of Nursie's list of potential hit men, Janet Murdo was not entirely certain he would agree.

'I shall go seek him,' she told the young woman, 'and if I get him not, I shall seek another. And if I get none, I shall do it myself.' Obviously, at least according to the ballads, Janet Murdo was determined that John Kincaid should be destined for the big sleep. But Lady Warriston held back. Robert Weir came to see her a number of times to discuss the problem, but she refused to speak with him. Finally, on Tuesday 1 July 1600, the terrible trio got together to flesh out the murder plot.

That night, Lady Warriston saw to it that her husband drank more than his usual share of wine. His senses thus dulled, he set off for bed and a night of drunken dreams. Robert Weir, meanwhile, had been hiding in the cellar and, after her husband retired for the night, Lady Jean came to him and led him through the house to the laird's bedchamber. Kincaid's sleep was not as sound as they would have liked for he woke when they came into the room and started to rise. Robert Weir, a strong man, leaped across the room and punched him on the jugular vein – or the 'vane-organ', as it is called in the later indictment. Kincaid fell from the bed and Weir slammed his booted foot down into his belly. The man cried out and the groom, fearing that the sound would be heard in other parts of the house, sat on his chest and wrapped his fingers round Kincaid's throat to ensure that any further noise would be stillborn. Kincaid kicked and struggled but the groom was too heavy for him. He clawed at the big hands round his neck but the man's grip was too tight for him. He lashed out at his attacker but Weir was too powerful to feel his puny blows. Finally, the movements beneath him slowed and dimmed until the body hung loosely from his hands, erupting blood vessels staining the whites of his bulging eyes pink, his tongue swollen and lolling from his mouth.

According to her own confession, given to a minister as she awaited execution, Lady Jean Warriston fled the room just as Robert Weir began to throttle her husband. She heard his stifled cries and groans but could listen or watch no more, so took refuge in the main hall, where the flames died in the grate as her husband's life ebbed away in the bedchamber. She waited there until Robert Weir came to her and said the deed was done. She wanted to go away with the groom, she said, but he refused. If the murder was not discovered, he told her, then she could say he died of natural causes; if it were uncovered, then he would flee the country and take the full blame. That, and the eagerness with which he embraced the murder plot, strongly suggests that there was something more between them.

The murder, however, was discovered but again, no one knows exactly how. At any rate, the following morning, Lady Jean Warriston, Janet Murdo and two other servants were arrested. Robert Weir, as soon as he heard, was as good as his word for he packed his bags and left in a marked manner. Lady Jean, meanwhile, tried to pretend to be a grieving wife.

'At first, that I might seem to be innocent, I laboured to counterfeit weeping,' she said, 'but do what I would, I could not find a tear.'

As the women had been taken 'red-hand', not quite with her fingers round her husband's throat but certainly within hours of the murder, the trial could be heard before the magistrates of Edinburgh. Statutes decreed that it must take place within three days of the crime being committed. Justice in those days was swift if not always thorough. When it was clear that her protestations of innocence were falling on deaf ears, Lady Jean moved to exonerate the two servants from any blame.

'They are both innocent and knew nothing of this deed before it was done,' she confessed. Although one of them was brought to trial with her, of the other nothing is known. William Roughead, in his account of the case, surmises that this woman agreed to give evidence against her mistress, either willingly to save her own skin or after the application of the 'Bootiekins' – a hugely popular but foul method of torture in which the foot was slowly crushed.

Lady Jean also attempted to get Janet Murdo off the hook but only served to make things worse when she said that 'when I told her what I was minded to do, she consented to the doing of it.' Her confession was made to the Rev. James Balfour, a local minister, who published it later under the title:

A Worthy and Notable Memorial of the Great Work of Mercy which God wrought in the Conversion of Jean Livingston, Lady Warriston, who was Apprehended for the Vile and Horrible Murder of her Own Husband, John Kincaid, committed on Tuesday July 1 1600, for which she was Execute on Saturday following. Containing an Account of her Obstinacy, Earnest Repentance, and her Turning to God; of the Odd Speeches she used during her Imprisonment; of her Great and Marvelous Constancy, and of her Behaviour and her Manner of Death, Observed by one who was both a Seer and Hearer of What was Spoken.

Of course, it will never be known how much of what is contained in that document was simply Balfour's interpretation of events. Certainly, it seems Lady Jean was unwilling to cleave to her religion at first, throwing the reverend's proffered bible against the wall and dismissing his preaching as 'trittle trattle'. But the Lady Jean of immediately after the murder was somewhat different from the Lady Jean who walked to The Maiden. In the hours after her arrest, she was in something of a rage and given to fits of temper. However, as she faced her death, she was calmer – a change attributed to her embracing her faith. According to Karl Marx, religion is the opium of the masses and Lady Jean had taken a lungful.

She came to trial on 3 July 1600. We do not know the form or extent of the evidence lodged against her or anything of the proceedings, such as they were. All we know is that she, Janet Murdo and the remaining servant were found guilty of the murder and were to be burned at the stake after first being 'wirreit' or strangled. She received the news calmly and with dignity. 'She never spoke one word, nor altered her countenance,' one eyewitness said later.

According to Rev. Balfour, her demeanour, after being sentenced, was a great change from the rage she had expressed before the trial. She had accepted her fate and was ready to deliver herself to her God. This dramatic transformation, though, was wrought only after thirty-seven straight hours of preaching from a total of fifteen ministers. Under such a barrage of homilies and exhortations to salvation, even the hardest of hearts would find it difficult to remain godless.

The nurse, though, was a different matter. Balfour found her to be 'very evil' and she wholeheartedly rejected his overtures, sending him scurrying back to Lady Jean, who was, by then, expressing a desire to see her baby son once more. At first the reverend and his colleagues were unwilling to allow this but they finally relented and the boy, who slept through the entire event, was brought to his mother's cell in the Edinburgh Tolbooth. She held him for the last time, kissed him tenderly on the head and then handed him back into the keeping of her dead husband's family.

Perhaps Lady Jean thought her father's influence would save her. After all, it was not unknown in Scottish justice for accused people to buy themselves out of trouble. But her father, for whatever reason, kept his distance from his condemned daughter. The only strings he pulled were in the manner and time of her death. Thanks to him, she was no longer to be 'wirreit' and burned but would, instead, meet her death on The Maiden, as befitted her station in life. And the execution would not take place, as was the custom, in the morning, but at a time when the great unwashed were unlikely to be abroad to witness it. However, the final decision as to when she would meet her doom was not shared with the young woman, leaving her in something of a limbo regarding her final preparations. Still, according to Rev. Balfour, she was now in a state of grace that shone from her like the sun. 'You give me many frights,' she told her jailers, 'but the Lord will not allow me to be afrighted.'

After another lengthy bout of praying and preaching, during

which she managed to snatch a few hours sleep, the magistrates attended Lady Jean Warriston. It was three in the morning of 5 July and she must have known immediately that her hour had come. For the first time, members of her family had come to see her and they showed an almost indecent haste in getting her out of the confines of the Tolbooth and on to The Maiden. Rev. Balfour was not pleased with this display of familial shame although his reasons were less out of anger for the woman's rejection than because he felt that they were depriving 'God's people of that comfort which they might have in this poor woman's death'. What comfort the populace might draw from seeing a twenty-year-old woman being beheaded is hard to see but, perhaps, he felt her bravery and new-found faith would be an example to them.

However, her family was having none of it. They wanted their disgraced relative dispatched quickly, quietly and with the minimum of publicity. And so, after her brother-in-law had given her a forgiving kiss, Lady Jean Warriston was led to the Girth Toll, at the foot of the Canongate, where The Maiden had been sited for the event.

A shiver ran through her slender frame as she gazed at the dark towers of the device and the blade glittering in the torchlight. Rev. Balfour reassured her that 'there was no death here, but a parting and entering into a better life'. This bolstered her spirits and she ascended the steps to the platform 'as cheerfully as if she had been going to her wedding and not her death'.

The family desire for a discreet end to the scandal was not to be for, despite the early hour, a large crowd turned out. She spoke to them from the four corners of the platform, confessing her crime. She asked Rev. Balfour to accompany her to the foot of The Maiden, which he did. She thanked him and asked for some further words of comfort, which he also did. Then, obviously moved, he left her to her fate. He could not bear to see the young woman for whom he had developed such admiration put to death.

She stood patiently while the blindfold was draped over her eyes, even providing a pin to fasten it. Then she calmly allowed herself to be laid down on the block. She tried twice to kneel but the hangman insisted she lie down so that he could pull her feet behind her in order to stretch her neck further. While a friend held her hand, she began to pray and the headsman pulled the lever that would set the blade slicing down. It fell only a few inches and Lady Jean continued to pray. However, just as she began to intone 'Into Thy hand, Oh Lord, I commend my soul', the blade swept down.

Janet Murdo and the poor servant – the latter no doubt had little, if anything, to do with the murder – met their ends at roughly the same time on Castle Hill. Their sentence remained unchanged for they were first strangled then their bodies burned at the stake, the smoke rising into the already lightening July sky.

Robert Weir remained on the run for four years. How he was arrested is unknown but he did come to trial on 26 June 1604. Naturally, he was found guilty but there was no easy death on The Maiden or stake for him. He was to be taken to a scaffold at Edinburgh's Cross and broken on the wheel. Although common on the continent, this was a highly unusual punishment in Britain. It had never happened in England and only once before in Scotland – in 1591, when a man was condemned for murdering his father. The horrific punishment saw Weir being bound to a cartwheel on a scaffold and then having every bone broken by the public hangman wielding 'a coulter of ane pleuch' – an iron cutting blade from a plough. His body was then left to hang on the wheel in a public place between Warriston and Leith as an example to others.

4

CORPSE AND ROBBERS

Helen Torrence and Jean Waldie, 1751-2

Scotland was not an easy place for surgeons to learn their trade although Scots are justifiably proud of their countrymen's achievements in medicine. Even the most casual glance down a list of pioneers reveals a host of surgeons and doctors from north of the Border who have been invaluable in furthering the cause of medical science. Among them are: brothers William and John Hunter, who distinguished themselves as surgeons; Sir James Young Simpson, who first determined the use of chloroform in the operating theatre; penicillin's discoverer, Sir Alexander Fleming; and James Syme, the first surgeon to recognise the advantages of anaesthetics.

But, for centuries, advances in medicine in Scotland were held back by the iron grip of the Kirk. It held to the belief that the body was governed by four elements – blood, phlegm and black and yellow bile – and that all maladies and distempers were rooted in one or more of these 'humours'. Any attempt to push the medical envelope was not just frowned upon but actively discouraged. Probing the mysteries of the body was considered a mortal sin and anatomists, who dissected human corpses, faced excommunication. According to the Church, the body had to be whole if it was to be resurrected come Judgement Day.

These religious scruples prevented would-be doctors from obtaining the raw materials they needed to explore and study the mysteries of human anatomy. Because many people believed there would be no afterlife if the body had been in any way violated, the medical profession was severely restricted with regard to the flesh and blood to which it was allowed to turn a scalpel. Students would practise their cutting techniques on the carcasses of animals but, obviously, this was not a perfect solution. They were also allowed the corpses of executed felons but really there wasn't enough of these cadavers to go round so they were often cut into separate sections to allow different students to practise various procedures on a single body. Naturally, this slice-and-dice school of surgery was far from perfect.

In Edinburgh in 1694, things were opened up a bit. Surgeons were allowed to use the bodies of foundlings who 'dye betwixt the time they are weaned and their being put to schools and trades'. They were also allowed the corpses of infants who had suffocated at birth, in addition, of course, to people who had found themselves at the wrong end of the gallows rope. A few years later, Aberdeen also allowed its surgeons the use of bodies of those who had died friendless and in the poor house.

However, as the number of medical students grew, so too did the demand for cadavers. Finally, students took matters into their own hands and adopted more covert ways of obtaining study tools. Some students did their own dirty work, creeping into graveyards in the dead of night armed with shovels and sacks. After some back-breaking digging, a recently interred corpse would be slung on to a cart and taken off to the dissecting rooms. However, the deceased's clothes were left behind because, although the lifting of a body was frowned upon, it was not exactly a crime – but removal of clothing would be considered theft.

Others, though, balked at the prospect of these midnight forays and found themselves forging unholy alliances with a new breed of criminal known as sack-em-up-boys, susie-lifters or resurrection-ists. The bodysnatching trade had been born. However, not all of these entrepreneurs restricted themselves to stealing the bodies of the dead. Some looked among the living for their subjects and the first case of this kind to come before the Scottish courts involved two women.

x x x

It was in the summer of 1751 that Edinburgh needlewoman Helen Torrence first offered a surgeon a cadaver. On this occasion, she was turned down as she was not a regular supplier and the young medical student, acting as a physician's assistant, did not fully trust her. However, he later regretted his decision – after all, a cadaver was a cadaver and even well-dressed and well-educated beggars could not be choosers – so, some months later, he offered to treat some sores on Torrence's leg in return for a body to be used for dissection. Torrence agreed, promising to have something for him the following day as her neighbour, Jean Waldie, was to perform a vigil over a dead child that very night. They would bribe the mother to let them take the corpse.

It all sounded very plausible and the student agreed. The only fly in Torrence's ointment, though, was that the child was not actually dead yet. Eight-year-old John Dallas was certainly sick, no doubt about it. He had suffered from the glandular condition, scrofula, for four years and the infection had left him deaf, speech-less and so weak that he was unable to leave home. But he was improving. His hearing was gradually returning and he was even learning to communicate through sign language.

His father really had no interest in anyone but himself and tended to leave the care of the child and the rest of the family to their mother, Janet Johnstone. Janet, though, was a drunkard and her judgement could be easily swayed by the liberal application of strong drink. It was this weakness that would lead to the death of her son.

With the Dallas boy rather inconsiderately remaining in the land of the living, Helen Torrence realised she had been a touch hasty in her promise of a corpse by the following day. When she did not show up with the agreed cadaver, two students turned up at her home in Fairlie's Close and demanded payment. She fobbed them off by telling them that the grieving mother had refused to part with her son's body and promised them another soon. The next day, Jean Waldie was recruited to tell the students that she and Torrence had possession of a body which was being stored in her home, also in Fairlie's Close. But she was under suspicion, she said, and needed some cash to leave the city until the heat died down. The students gave her some cash and visited Helen Torrence again and she assured them of the existence of the body but – wouldn't you just know it – she could not get into Jean's home.

Of course, there was no body and, by this time, the women were aware they had talked themselves into a corner. A body would have to be found and preferably a young one.

Helen Torrence hit on the notion that young John Dallas be taken from his home in Stonielaw Close and carried to Fairlie's Close. In his condition, she reasoned, he would be dead before the journey's end. So the two women hatched a plot to keep the boy's mother occupied while Jean Waldie kidnapped the child. Janet Johnstone had asked Torrence to make a shirt for her youngest son and was offered a drink when she came to collect it. Just to be sociable, she accepted the proffered grog. And another. And another. She was a very sociable person. Jean Waldie, meanwhile, had pleaded illness and retired to her own room upstairs so Helen, good friend that she was, felt duty bound to check on her every now and then, leaving Janet alone with the bottle. On one of these 'trips upstairs', Torrence nipped over to Janet's rooms to check that the coast was clear for Waldie to snatch the lad.

With Torrence once more back keeping the bibulous Janet Johnstone company, Waldie enticed John Dallas from his bed and into the night. As Helen predicted, by the time he reached Fairlie's Close, the weak little boy was dead.

The women had agreed a deposit of 2 shillings and 10 pence for the body, plus a further 3 shillings when the students came to collect it. However, they were unable to hide the corpse safely so Torrence – a big, strong woman – wrapped it in her apron and carried it herself to the room of the physician's apprentice, Andrew Anderson. It was stored under the bed and she received another sixpence for her trouble. All in all, it was a profitable night's work for the two women.

Meanwhile, Janet Johnstone had weaved her way home and

found the youngster's bed empty. Her husband was furious when he heard she had been out drinking with cronies, while their son was being spirited away, and threw her out. Naturally, she turned to her pal Helen Torrence who, fine Christian woman that she was, took her in.

It was while she was staying with Torrence that the worried mother witnessed an argument over money between her hostess and Jean Waldie. Torrence spun her a yarn about making an apron, paid for by Waldie's husband, but Janet Johnstone, her mind now clear, remained unconvinced. She began to make some discreet inquiries and discovered that Waldie's husband had never paid up front for an apron. But, more damning, was a neighbour who had spotted Torrence near Stonielaw Close on the night young John had disappeared – and had actually had a conversation with her.

Word spread through the tenements that Helen Torrence had kidnapped the Dallas boy although no one yet knew he was dead and lying under the bed of a medical student. It was not there for long though. The physician's apprentices moved it to an empty room in the Cowgate where it was laid on a slab and prepared for dissection. By the time news of the abduction and Torrence's alleged involvement reached the doctors and students, they had already sliced the little body open along the lower abdomen and were preparing for further probing. They realised they had been party to child murder so they hastily sewed the guts together again before dumping the corpse somewhat unceremoniously in a close off Libberton's Wynd.

Torrence and Waldie were quickly arrested and promptly blamed each other for the murder. This did them no good whatsoever as they were both found guilty of murder and sentenced to hang. Torrence attempted to escape the noose by claiming she was pregnant but close examination by a team of midwives proved this to be a ruse so she and her accomplice were led to the gallows on the Grassmarket on 18 March 1752.

On the scaffold, Waldie repented her crimes but continued to heap the blame on her erstwhile pal's shoulders. She said she had been drunk when Torrence talked her into the plan, claiming the young Dallas boy must have smothered under her clothes as she carried him through the streets. However, she agreed her execution was warranted since she had been responsible. Torrence, though, merely warned the spectators against the perils of 'drunkenness, bad company and uncleanliness'. The noose was then placed around their necks and the first two convicted bodysnatching killers were launched into eternity.

The death of John Dallas and the execution of the two women were tragic and the case shocked Edinburgh. However, the real horror was to come nearly eighty years later (*see* 'Distaff of Legend', pp. 77–96) but a family scandal and a daring escape from the notorious Edinburgh Tolbooth would rock Scotland first.

5

HISTORY WRAPPED
IN AN ENIGMA

Katharine Nairn, 1765

He stood on the gallows platform, a chill breeze plucking at his clothes and his hair. Despite the cold, despite the stares of the gathering crowd, he held himself proudly and looked back at the people who had come to this place to see justice served and to gawp at his final moments.

But, if they were expecting to see him flinch or to turn craven, they were to be disappointed – for he was a soldier of the Crown, an officer and a gentleman. And, in his own mind, he was something more important – he was innocent of the foul crime of which he had been convicted.

However, if he entertained any thoughts of escape or of being liberated by his messmates, then he was the one who was to be disappointed for the authorities had his regiment penned up in Edinburgh Castle until due process of law had been observed. His co-accused, at that moment sitting in a cell in the city's Tolbooth, had other ideas, though. She had been found guilty of murdering her husband and of enjoying an incestuous relationship with the proud officer standing on the gallows. But there would be no death procession to the Grassmarket for her, no anxious moments on the platform as the noose was draped around her lovely neck, no gasps from the crowd as she was turned off to jerk and strain at the rope. Pregnancy had already granted her a respite and she planned a more permanent liberation. However, for the man facing the drop that morning – proclaiming his innocence to the mob – death was inevitable. But not swift.

At nineteen, Katharine Nairn was a beauty much admired by many men in and around her home at Glen Isla in what is now Angus. It was said that her charms had proved painful for at least one suitor but fatal for another. One story tells of two young men who had fought a duel for her favours, their swords clanging in the crisp air as the object of their desire looked on. A passing shepherd said that, when one of them fell to the hard earth and the winner refused to finish him off, Miss Nairn herself stepped forward and plunged a dagger into the poor man's back. The swordsman, still standing, tried to stop her but was himself attacked for his pains.

This wounded lover did not die but another would-be husband was not so fortunate – he was found dead at the foot of a cliff. It is possible that this romancer had been rebuffed by the beautiful young woman and, in a fit of dramatic remorse, had thrown himself off the precipice. Or, given later events, we may wonder if he had got in the way of her ambitions. In other words, did he fall or was he pushed? However, it was the mysterious death of the man who finally did win her hand that brought lasting notoriety for Katharine Nairn.

There was great surprise in 1765 when Katharine agreed to marry Thomas Ogilvy, Laird of Eastmiln. Given the vast interest in her hand from other, younger, men it might seem strange that she chose to marry the forty-year-old landowner. But life was different in those days and daughters were required to marry well. If there was affection between the two parties, then all the better but it was not a prerequisite. Sir Thomas Nairn, Katharine's father, was no different. Ogilvy of Eastmiln was settled and he came from good stock – although one brother had committed suicide and another, Alexander, had the effrontery to marry 'beneath him' by taking the hand of a porter's daughter. Despite this, it was felt that Thomas Ogilvy would be a steadying influence on Sir Thomas Nairn's somewhat headstrong, some may even say wayward, lass.

And so, on 30 January 1765, Katharine Nairn became Katharine Ogilvy and took up residence in the family home near Forfar.

Although the family had money, they were not grand lairds in the accepted sense. Eastmiln House was not a large mansion and was comprised of only two floors. At ground level, there were two rooms – a parlour and the kitchen where the servants not only worked but slept – and, on the upper floor, there were just two bedrooms. At first Katharine settled easily and even willingly into her new role as wife and lady of the house. Her husband seemed to be in poor health and she dutifully ministered to him. Her influence was good and it was noted that Ogilvy cast off the shabby clothing he was in the habit of wearing and became, if not dapper, at least smarter in appearance. But it was not long before things began to change.

William Roughead's account of the case pinpoints the date of change to the day Ogilvy's cousin, Anne Clark, arrived at the house. According to Roughead, her character was not what you might call exemplary. In fact, he calls her a downright liar and of dubious virtue although he couches it in his own elegant fashion by saying that 'her private character and professional pursuits, if known, would necessarily have excluded her from decent society'. Those professional pursuits had been of late shared with Alexander Ogilvy, the family's black sheep. Some of them, it has been suggested, may even have been of an incestuous nature. In March 1765, she arrived at Eastmiln, ostensibly to engineer a rapprochement between the two brothers although she may have had a more sinister motive. Alexander was in need of cash but there was little likelihood of him inheriting the family fortune. For one thing, now that Thomas had taken himself a young and vibrant wife, there was every chance he would have a son. And, even if there was no issue, there was Patrick to consider.

Patrick was another Ogilvy brother serving as a lieutenant with the 89th Regiment of Foot. He had recently been invalided back to Scotland from India and been given one of the two bedrooms at Eastmiln. Anne, meanwhile, bunked with Lady Eastmiln in a box-bed in the parlour. Patrick would already have caught the eye of his brother's beautiful Katharine, whose own recent past revealed a weakness for good-looking young men. Perhaps Anne, with a sixth sense for such chemistry, hit on the plan to bring the two young people together, thus preventing any future son and heir – and discrediting Patrick at the same time.

Whatever the truth, whispers began to slide around the corridors of Eastmiln that the young mistress's affections for her brother-in-law were something more than sisterly. Always at the hub of these rumours was Anne Clark, like a gleeful spider tugging at the strands of a web. She claimed to have solid evidence proving Katharine's indiscretions – although, given the cramped nature of the living environment, they were unlikely to consummate their affections in the house itself. But there was plenty of room on the estate – and a barn was always a popular place for a roll in the hay.

Despite her gossiping, Anne apparently befriended Katharine and claimed the young woman confided in her that, not only did she have no love for her husband, she also actively wished him dead. According to Anne, Katharine more than once expressed a desire 'to give him a dose' – not of some sexual disease, which would have been bad enough, especially in the days before penicillin, but of poison. She inquired as to where she might buy some substance, perhaps on the pretence of poisoning rats (a poisoner's favourite) but Anne, it seems, offered to have her own brother in Edinburgh obtain it. This was never done but, eventually, Katharine and Patrick would take matters into their own hands.

Meanwhile, the Chinese whispers regarding his wife's infidelity had reached the ears of the laird and, when Patrick raised the subject of a family allowance, Thomas hit back by accusing his brother of cuckolding him under his own roof. Enraged or embarrassed, Patrick stormed out of the house and took up residence with friends close by. The laird, obviously not convinced by cousin Anne's rumour-mongering, soon thought better of this hot-headedness and asked his young brother to return but Patrick refused. In fact, he was already taking the first steps towards the gallows. At Katharine's request, he obtained laudanum from a doctor friend and almost an ounce of arsenic – the former for Katharine's use and the latter, ostensibly, to put down some dogs that were playing havoc with the local sporting life by being let loose to harass game. When Patrick's brother-in-law, Andrew Stewart, declared his intention to visit Eastmiln, Patrick, after rifling through some articles in his sea chest recently delivered from Dundee, gave him a small glass phial of liquid and a paper packet of 'salts' and asked him to hand them directly to Katharine.

Katharine, in the meantime, was continuing her dialogue with Anne Clark, confiding in her that Patrick had obtained the necessary poisons and was sending them to her. Anne said she did her best to dissuade the young woman from this homicidal course of action. Katharine, though, was apparently heart-set on doing away with the now inconvenient Mr Ogilvy and setting up house with the dashing young officer – if not at home, then perhaps abroad.

Anne Clark seemed determined, at least in her own words, to prevent the foul murder from taking place. First she waylaid Andrew Stewart and told him outright of the young woman's plans. Naturally, the man was shocked by the news but he also knew of Anne's reputation and, as he had already handed the laudanum and salts to Katharine, ignored the warning. Anne next turned to Lady Eastmiln, Thomas's mother, but she remained unimpressed by her dire warnings. Finally, she spoke to Eastmiln himself but he, knowing her too well, also took her words with a pinch of salt. Or, as we shall see, more than a pinch of salts.

Andrew Stewart, however, soon had his eyes opened. After a dinner at Kirkton of Glen Isla, he found himself in Katharine's company as they made their way home and was stunned to hear her say how unhappy she was and that she wished her husband, or herself, dead. Later that night he suggested to Lady Eastmiln and Anne Clark that they break open the chest in which Katharine had stored the articles he had delivered but neither woman agreed. Thomas's mother later declared that she had already listened at the door of her son's bedroom and heard him talking with his young wife. She had noted there 'was more kindness between them than usual', which means that either they were talking pleasantly or it was a euphemism for sex. Whatever was going on in that room that night, it would be the last time Thomas Ogilvy would do it.

During the night, the Laird took ill and so was unable to come down for breakfast the following morning. Katharine, being a dutiful wife, poured him some tea, complete with milk and sugar, and took it upstairs to him. Anne, on hearing this, began to worry that the young woman had decided to follow through her murderous plans – with some justification, it seems, for, later that morning, Ogilvy turned very ill indeed. Andrew Stewart, who witnessed some of the vomiting, wanted to call a doctor but Katharine resisted, saying her husband would recover soon. Eventually she gave in but her husband did indeed rally enough to attend to some business. However, within a few hours, he was struck down again. Carried to his bed, he was unable to hold down anything he ate or drank, and complained of serious heartburn, diarrhoea, desperate thirst and pains in his legs. The symptoms only eased when Anne Clark gave him a glass of wine with some sugar in it, although she later said that the wine had come from Katharine. When offered a drink of water from the same bowl in which Katharine had given him tea that morning, he refused, saying, 'Damn that bowl – for I have got my death in it already.' Servants said he was convinced his wife had poisoned him and one recalled seeing Mrs Ogilvy stirring something into the brew that morning. However, she did not see her actually put anything into the bowl so it was possible all the young woman was doing was stirring the milk and sugar she had placed in it downstairs. It appears many of the servants had swallowed Anne Clark's stories for they were ready to claim that Mrs Ogilvy prevented anyone from seeing her husband even though this was patently untrue. Five people visited the Laird as he lay ill, including neighbours and a local minister.

Before that day – Thursday 6 June – had ended, Thomas Ogilvy of Eastmiln was dead. He died in pain. He died vomiting. He died convinced his wife had done for him.

The doctor finally arrived but hazarded no opinion as to what had killed the man. He did, however, talk with the new, already grieving, widow who asked him to 'conceal from the world' what he might think had been the cause of death. Patrick, meanwhile, had rushed to the house on hearing of his brother's illness and, on being challenged by Anne Clark over supplying the poison, said he did not think Katharine 'had so barbarous a heart that she would use it.'

Despite her suspicions, Anne claimed she kept her own counsel, possibly out of familial loyalty but more likely because Katharine gave her some cash. Someone did, however, tell Alexander Ogilvy that his brother's death was far from natural. During the funeral, a week later on 11 June, he staged a dramatic entrance and brought the proceedings to a halt, demanding that investigations be made. This naturally upset Katharine, either because she was being prevented from laying her husband to rest or because, in fact, she had murdered him. Meanwhile a friend, knowing the rumours, advised Patrick to flee. Patrick, insisting he was innocent, opted to stay.

A post-mortem was organised for the following day but it never took place because, amazingly, none of the assigned doctors were present at the same time. Two doctors viewed the body together but they refused to open it without the third being present. The latter arrived late and then also refused to do any cutting because he feared that this might somehow endanger his own life! All three medical men, therefore, contented themselves with an external examination of the corpse.

Alexander, though, was not letting the grass grow under his feet. He lodged an official complaint, accusing Katharine and Patrick of murder. Then, after they were arrested and locked up in Forfar Gaol, he and his dear cousin, Anne, looted the estate. This was carried out by fraudulent means because, although he was locked up on charges of murder, Patrick was still the legal heir.

Alexander, being as honest as an Arctic winter day is long, forged a letter of authority and promptly sold all the estate's sheep and cattle at auction.

This mattered little to Patrick, though. Breaching the commandment 'Thou shalt not kill' was viewed seriously enough – unless it was broken in the name of religion or the state. But, in a society dominated by the Kirk, the commandment 'Thou shalt not commit adultery' was much more powerful – and he had committed more than that mortal sin with the comely Katharine. As she was his sister-in-law, he was also guilty of incest. Blood kin they were not but the law prohibited them from having any kind of relations with members of the wider family and the term 'wider' at the time was very wide indeed. In 1569, a man was hanged because he had had an affair with his uncle's girlfriend. While, in 1626, another was beheaded after he married the widow of his stepmother's brother. Clearly, then, the courts would take a dim view of any indiscretions committed by Katharine and Patrick.

They were moved from Forfar to Edinburgh's Tolbooth, the infamous Heart of Midlothian near St Giles' Cathedral. Word of their alleged crimes preceded them and Katharine was met by an angry mob as she stepped ashore at Leith. They had expected to see a frightened young woman but, instead, they got a confident, vivacious young beauty, laughing with the sailors who ferried her across the Forth. This only inflamed the crowd's passions even more and they would probably have lynched her there and then had the authorities not managed to force her through the throng and on to Edinburgh.

In Scotland, until 1898, an accused person was prevented from giving evidence in court so pre-trial judicial examinations were viewed as all-important. In these declarations, the accused was able to present his or her side of the story – but heaven help them if what they claimed proved to be false in any way. Katharine's examination was simple: she didn't do it; the laudanum and salts were for her own use; she did not put anything untoward in her dead husband's tea; that, in fact, he did not finish it and the remainder was given to a servant, who was also feeling poorly that morning. There was some evidence to back up her story. Servants, suspicious of greasiness at the bottom of the bowl in question, had 'tested' it by feeding a dog some broth from it. The dog survived. The sickly servant admitted receiving tea from Katharine on the morning in question but did not believe it to be in the same bowl. As for Katharine's claim that she took the salts for medicinal purposes only, it was true she was in delicate health at the time, a fact that would become very important in the weeks to come.

But poor Patrick made the mistake of lying in his examination, claiming he did not obtain any substances for Katharine. Unfortunately for him, the doctor from whom he had bought them told a different story. The medical man confirmed he had given Patrick a quantity of laudanum and what may have been arsenic, although he could not swear to the exact nature of the latter substance. All he could say was that he had sold it to others and that it had been singularly effective in disposing of rats. But the damage had been done to Patrick's case. He tried to amend his examination but these things were binding.

The trial began on Monday 5 August 1765 although evidence was not heard until the following Monday 12 August. Beginning at 7 a.m., the case would continue unchecked until a verdict was heard. Anne Clark, as the principal prosecution witness, had proved somewhat slippery so had been kept under lock and key in Edinburgh Castle. It seems she was happy to repeat everything to anyone but was backward in coming forward to tell the court under oath. Unfortunately, as Roughead tells us, she was kept in the same room as three of the servants, also prosecution witnesses. The temptation for the four women to discuss their evidence would have been too much and memories would no doubt have been embellished with the telling. Katharine had even dismissed one of these servants from the family's service for theft but this was not seen as a hurdle to giving evidence against the accused. Scottish prosecutors were willing to overlook any crime as long as the witness was saying what they wanted.

There were no scientific methods of detecting poison in those days so the opinion of doctors was all the courts had to go by regarding cause of death. The fact that there had not even been a post-mortem was not seen as a major problem. One doctor found that the deceased's nails were discoloured and his tongue was swollen and stuck to the roof of his mouth. The doctor admitted he had no experience of poisons but said that the victim's brother, Alexander, had suggested that it was death by poisoning and that seemed good enough for him. Another doctor also remarked on the discolouration of the lips but both men admitted they had also seen similar symptoms in natural deaths. The third medico spoke about blotches on the arms and legs but this was more likely to have been due to the body lying unburied for a number of days. The medical evidence, therefore, was inconclusive.

Although Anne and the servants were willing to swear Thomas Ogilvy had been a hale and hearty man, this was not the case. He had never been a strong man, it seems, and, prior to his death, he had been exhibiting signs of sickness – even before Katharine had received the laudanum and salts from Patrick. However, for some reason the court did not hear evidence concerning the dead man's ongoing state of health from his mother who could easily have clarified this particular point.

Most of the evidence was circumstantial. There was no scientific proof, no real eyewitness evidence. The Crown's star witness was a lady whose repute was not so much ill but dead and mouldering in the grave. Another, the sacked servant, had an axe to grind against Katharine. But Katharine herself had admitted asking Patrick to obtain the laudanum and salts – and it had been proved that Patrick had not only bought them but had lied about it in his judicial examination.

The trial itself was, by modern standards, little more than a farce. In total, thirty-three hours were spent hearing the prosecution's side but only three hearing the defence – the gentlemen of the jury were simply not interested in hearing this. Roughead stated it was common, during this case, for the jury to wander about the room and discuss matters with the prosecution witnesses and counsel. And food and drink were brought into the courtroom at will. This is not surprising considering that the hearing carried on from the Monday until Wednesday without any breaks – apart from those for calls of nature. The case began with three judges listening on the bench but, at some point during the middle of the proceedings, there was only one – his two colleagues were off discussing matters with some jury members and opposing counsel.

According to Roughead, the case also marked the first time that a judge in Scotland indulged in a spot of summing up. Until then it was customary for the final word on the matter to come from the accused's advocate but, in this case, one of the judges, Lord Kames, spoke to the jury, providing a summary of what had gone before. This was already done as a matter of course in sheriff courts but it would not be enshrined in law until 1783 for more serious cases. Courts kept few records and, by and large, the only official outline of the evidence was contained in the judges' notes so a run-down of the evidence for and against was vital to the bleary-eyed jury. The problem was that Scottish justice could be notoriously one-sided and the danger arose that a judge could favour the prosecution in his closing speech.

With all of this going on, it was not surprising that, at 4 p.m. on the Wednesday, the jury returned verdicts of guilty on both accused. The death sentence was duly announced, with Patrick consigned to go to the gallows on 25 September. But Katharine won herself a respite from dancing the hangman's jig – that delicate health for which she had needed the salts was in fact an advanced pregnancy. It is open to question who the father was but, by 'pleading her belly', she was able to put off her date with the rope until after the birth. But, as we shall see, other forces were at work to postpone that date indefinitely.

Despite attempts to show that the trial was far from fair, Patrick failed to have his sentence quashed or commuted. Three separate dates were set for his execution and each one was put off while friends and supporters tried new ways to expose the shambles of the Scottish court. During that time, he remained in his cell in the Tolbooth, honing his skills as a fiddler to pass the time. However,

Scottish courts – even now – are loath to admit they were wrong and he was finally taken from the Tolbooth to the Grassmarket where the gallows stood. He spoke to the crowd, declaring in a clear voice that he was innocent of the crimes of which he had been convicted and that 'no persuasion could ever have made me condescend to them'.

But his trials were not yet over. As he was turned from the gallows, the noose gave way and he fell to the ground. Justice, though, would not be denied. He was grabbed roughly by the hangman and others and forced back up on to the platform. This time the noose held and he dangled there until he was slowly throttled to death. A member of the Society of Tron-men, or chimney sweeps, was banished from the organisation for assisting in this incident and was sent to Leith for five years. It's unrecorded which of the punishments the Edinburgh man thought worse.

Meanwhile, Katharine reclined in her own cell, supping twice a day on ale, double rum, white wine and tea until her pregnancy ran to term. She was visited regularly by midwives, in particular a Mrs Shiells or Shields who, for some of the time, was apparently suffering severe toothache and had her head wrapped in a scarf. On 27 January 1766, the prisoner gave birth to a daughter. Two months later, in the strange way the law looks at things, the court debated whether the condemned woman was strong enough to have her death sentence completed. It was decided to put off the final judgement for a further seven days.

As it turned out, the decision was taken out of their hands. On Saturday 15 March, Katharine walked out of her Tolbooth cell and disappeared into the night. She was either dressed as a man or as Mrs Shiells, the toothache-suffering midwife with the scarf covering her face. Whatever the truth, it is almost certain that money changed hands. Katharine's uncle was the lawyer William Nairn, then Commissary Clerk of Edinburgh but later made Lord Dunsinnan and promoted to judge. It is believed he used his good offices – and part of his fortune – to oil the hinges of the escape by greasing the palms of the turnkeys.

Once free of the Tolbooth, Katharine hid in the cellar of her uncle's house until the coast was sufficiently clear for her to be spirited out of the city in the company of her uncle's loyal clerk. She was taken by carriage to Dover – this time, they say, disguised as an army officer, complete with cocked and plumed hat. The authorities offered two rewards of £100 each for her capture but these went unclaimed.

She left her infant daughter behind in the Tolbooth but the child did not remain there for long. She died in that foul place at two months old, apparently having been smothered – how or by whom is unknown. With Patrick hanged and Katharine a fugitive from justice, the way was now clear for the remaining brother, Alexander, to take possession of what was left of the Eastmiln estate. But things were not to work out as he had planned. He was arrested in March for bigamy and subsequently banished for seven years. However, before he was due to leave the country, he leaned too far out of an Edinburgh window and fell to his death. Of his erstwhile partner in crime, Anne Clark, nothing much is known.

But what of the beautiful Katharine Nairn? After her escape from the Tolbooth, she slips into legend. They say she went to France and managed to survive the revolution of 1789 before travelling to America and giving birth to a large family. Another version has her continuing to kill in France although this does seem unlikely. Yet another holds that she married a Dutchman and lived a long and happy life. She may also have taken herself to a nunnery but eventually made her way to England where she died.

Did she murder Thomas Ogilvy? Given the paucity of evidence, it is difficult to say. Anne Clark's claims that Katharine told her of her unhappiness and her murderous plans must be taken with a full handful of snuff. Yet Katharine did ask Patrick to obtain the poisons, which he duly did, although it is probable he did not know to what purpose they might be put. The authorities would also point to her escape as an admission of guilt, as an attempt to flee justice. An attempt to flee it most certainly was but it could just as easily have been from an unjust conviction as a flight from guilt. At the time of her flight, she was still a young woman and to have had her life ended for a murder she did not commit – if there was a murder – would have been a crime. She left her newly born daughter in the Tolbooth but history does not record whether she did so with a cold or a heavy heart. It would certainly have been difficult to smuggle the child out – although, if the guards had been paid off as has been suggested, surely they would have turned a blind eye to the infant too. If the woman was a murderer, then the child was her youngest victim.

Katharine Nairn is one of the most complex of Scotland's wicked women. Angel or devil, saint or sinner, innocent or guilty – hers is a case of history wrapped in an enigma.

6

DISTAFF OF LEGEND

Helen McDougall and Maggie Laird, 1828

Scotland is only a small country but it has many cases of murder that continue to excite the imagination and send gallons of printer's ink flowing like blood across acres of paper. The story of Madeleine Smith is one of everlasting mystery. The trial of Oscar Slater, wrongly convicted of murder in Glasgow, is one of everlasting shame. Peter Manuel is, perhaps, the most terrifying – not only did he target young girls walking alone he also crept into the homes of innocent people and slaughtered everyone he found. Shadowy Bible John, who may have killed at least three women, still haunts the minds of Glaswegians. But, of all the oft-repeated tales of murder, both single and mass, two notorious names resound through the decades and echo around the world. Their crimes are at the centre of the first properly documented cases of multiple murder in the country and simply naming them conjures up images of a dark and noisome city, of conspiracy and cover-up, of deprivation and decay and death. They are, of course, Burke and Hare.

They have been called bodysnatchers and resurrectionists but they were not. The moonlight trade of grave robbing was not for them. They found an easier way to provide their favoured anatomist, Robert Knox, with study tools and, at the same time, line their own pockets. Murder was their trade and business was brisk. Their death tally has been placed at as high as thirty but the most commonly accepted figure is sixteen – with all the deaths occurring within a period of a few months.

They did not work alone, however. What is often sidelined in popular retellings of the tale is that there were two other people involved. They were with the men during the killing time and, although they may not have been involved in the actual murders, they did benefit from them.

Helen McDougall and Maggie Laird were, respectively, the wives – if only by bad habit and ill repute – of Burke and Hare. And they were up to their necks in those dark deeds of 1828 Edinburgh.

Of the principal dancers in the ballet of death that was to follow, only Helen McDougall was a Scot, born in Redding near Falkirk. She had once been an attractive woman but the life of a poor woman in early nineteenth-century Scotland had taken its toll on her features. However, when news of the mass murder hit the newspapers, she was described as still being 'tolerably good-looking'. She had taken her surname from that of a man she had once lived with and was already the mother of two children when she turned to prostitution. What happened to her offspring is unknown. Perhaps they stayed with their natural father, perhaps they were sent out for adoption or perhaps they died. If life was hard for adults in those days, it was brutal for the young.

Around 1818–19, the countryside around Falkirk was teeming with Irishmen who had come to Scotland to eke a hard living out of digging the Union Canal, which would link the Forth and Clyde waterways with Edinburgh in the east. It was back-breaking work but the men, the famed Irish navvies, had fled the dire poverty of their homeland in search of employment. They were hard workers and, more importantly for the employers, they were cheap. This, of course, did not endear them to the native workforce who often saw them as subhuman.

With human nature and the sex drive being what they are, wherever there are large bodies of men living away from home, there are always going to be women who are ready to see to their needs – for a price. Helen McDougall was one such woman and it was during this time that she met the young Irishman, William Burke. He had left his home, complete with wife and two children, in County Tyrone to seek his fortune but all he found was the sweat and strain of working in the ditches. Helen McDougall must have been attracted to the squat little Irishman, with the piercing dark eyes and his love of dancing, for he first became a client, then a regular and, finally, her one and only. Despite his tendency to slap her around, there appeared to be some genuine feeling between the two – even while he was languishing in the condemned cell in Edinburgh, Burke sought to excuse her from his litany of death.

After four years of working on the canal, the pair dodged around central Scotland and, by 1827, found themselves in Edinburgh, repairing and dealing in second-hand boots and shoes. One day, in the street, they met an Irish woman called Maggie Laird who was known to Burke. The two had become three.

One contemporary chronicler deliciously describes Laird as 'a poor, miserable, boney, skinny, scranky, wizened jade'. Clearly she was not as attractive as 'Nelly' McDougall but she was just as free with her favours. Unlike Nell, though, she did not take it up professionally. Maggie was a tough piece and had laboured on the canal herself, wielding a pick and shovel and digging out the hard Scottish earth with the best of them. Once she set aside her spade, she took up with a man called Logue who ran a down-at-heel lodging house in Tanner's Close, in the area off the Grassmarket known as the West Port. Lodging house is a grand name for what Logue – and many others like him – provided in the filthy, stinking Old Town. Basically, he charged for a leaking roof, a bed of dirty straw, that could be shared by up to three people, and all the lice they could kill. If customers did not like what was offered, they could move on and God damn their eyes for there was seldom a shortage of people looking for somewhere to lay their heads for a few pence a night. The ragged and the filthy, the poor and the desperate, the honest and the crooked – they were all flooding into the nation's cities in search of a new life or work or simply a place to hide.

By the time Laird had met up with Burke and McDougall in the street, Logue had died and she had a new squeeze – a man named

William Hare. Hare had also come over from Ireland to graft on the Union Canal and, like the man who was soon to become his partner in crime, had gravitated towards Edinburgh where he found labouring work and a bed in Logue's house. It was here that he had first met Maggie although it is possible that, like Burke, he had known her while working on the canal. The two took a fancy to each other and Hare was soon giving her something more than a thrupenny bit each night. They were a well-matched pair for she was no prize and he was far from the answer to a maiden's prayer – even though Maggie had not been a maiden for many a long year. One contemporary description states the lanky Hare had 'dull, blackish, dead eyes' and 'a coarse-lipped mouth' which, mixed with his high cheekbones and sunken cheeks, inspired 'disgust and abhorrence, so utterly loathsome was the whole look of the reptile'.

Naturally, Logue had taken a dim view of the liaison between his woman and the newcomer so he had sent Hare packing. But, after the landlord died, Hare was back under the roof and in Maggie Laird's bed. He, like Burke, was a bit too free with his fists when it came to women and it is said that Laird was often seen sporting a pair of black eyes.

And so, during the street conversation and subsequent visit to a tavern, Burke told Laird that he and Helen planned leaving Edinburgh for the west country, where Burke hoped to set up business as a cobbler. Laird suggested they lodge in Tanner's Court for a while. There was a room available there, she said, and perhaps Burke could try his luck in Edinburgh. There they met William Hare, now styling himself as a landlord. And, thus, the three became four.

Burke and Hare – both Irishmen, both former navvies – seemed to bond immediately. They made an incongruous pair – Hare was tall and cadaverous, the archetypal ghoul, and Burke was short and thick-set with an air of respectability. But, for the women, it was another matter. Maggie Laird never fully trusted Helen McDougall. Perhaps it was a racial thing for Helen was Scottish and many Irish people, particularly Irish Catholics, had first-hand experience of prejudice at the hands of the natives – the flame lit by John Knox was still burning brightly. Perhaps Maggie did not like the idea of having a former prostitute under her roof. Or perhaps she had an eye for Burke herself for it would appear he was the better-looking of the two men – but then, compared to Hare, Quasimodo would have been a matinee idol.

Business boomed in the lodging house for every day there seemed to be a new influx of transients flooding the city. They joined the thousands living in the tall tenements that clustered round the castle like ticks on a stray dog. They filled the many taverns and drinking dens that lined the roads and alleys. They clogged the streets, wading through the sewage that ran openly in the gutters and dodging the fresh filth tossed from the windows above. Death and disease walked hand in hand here and often stepped into the overcrowded lodging houses. It was sickness that would give the new friends their first item of merchandise for butcher Robert Knox.

In November 1827, with Burke and McDougall ensconced in Tanner's Close, an old soldier named Donald had the audacity to die while owing landlord Hare the sum of £4. Hare was not the fellow to let such a debt go uncollected so the body was howked out of the coffin as it lay awaiting burial and sacks of bark put in its place. It was well known that doctors paid handsomely for fresh cadavers so Hare suggested they cart old Donald round to Surgeon's Square and see what they could get for him. In the end, they received over £7 from the well-respected Dr Robert Knox. Before they left his premises, Burke and Hare were told that, should they have any further bodies to dispose of, the surgeons would be happy to see them again. Heading back to Tanner's Close, the two would probably have discussed how they might obtain such goods. It would be realised very early on that they could not simply wait around for tenants to die – and the idea of stealing into graveyards in the middle of the night to rob graves was not one that appealed to them. They'd had enough of digging during their years on the canal, thank you very much. After a couple of months of inactivity, they reached the conclusion that there was only one way they could guarantee a steady supply of such merchandise. They would just have to kill the people themselves.

The correct order of the murders is not known for certain. The next victim was either an old tenant named Joseph, a nameless Englishman or a woman named Abigail Simpson. Joseph's situation was most inconvenient for his landlords because he had developed a fever and, if word of sickness in the house got out, they could lose their business. Their tenants may not have been too choosy but they were not stupid enough to leave themselves open to infection. Joseph was also proving tardy in actually dying so, after some discussion – in which Laird may well have been involved – it was decided to put Joseph out of his misery. The old, sickly man was first made insensible with whisky and then smothered, Hare's hand clamped over his nose and mouth, Burke's body draped across his chest to keep him still and to prevent him from making any noise that may alert the other tenants. In subsequent murders, they swapped their roles – one would smother, the other sit on the victim's chest – but the end result was always the same and Dr Knox had a fresh and unmarked corpse ready for the cutting. Little did they know that they had recreated the murder method used by Robert Weir over two hundred years earlier when disposing of Jean Livingston's husband (*see* 'Death and the Maiden', pp. 49–56). Their modus operandi later became known as 'Burking'.

Plying their victims with liquor also became a vital part of their routine. Maggie Laird may also have taken a more active role by enticing intended victims into their slaughterhouse. She was certainly with Hare when they met elderly Abigail Simpson. The pair got her drunk and lured her back to Tanner's Close where he and Burke duly killed her. The Englishman, like Joseph, was a tenant who fell ill and had to be removed. For each of the cadavers they received £10, a far from paltry amount in those days. Hare took half but Burke received only £4. The remaining pound went into Maggie Laird's greedy little hand. After all, it was reasoned, the work was being done under her roof.

Whatever the order of death, they were getting away with murder. There was no outcry over the disappearance of these unfortunates. They were the lost and the lonely and no one seemed to notice they were even missing. That was until Burke selected the good-looking prostitute, Mary Paterson, as his next victim – and, for the first time, Helen McDougall was known to have played a part.

Teenage Mary and her friend, Janet Brown, met William Burke in a city tavern where they had dropped in for an early morning 'tightener', having spent the night in the lock-up for a breach of the peace. He chatted the pair of them up and invited them back to the home of his brother, Constantine, in Gibb's Close, off the Canongate. At this stage, he may have had nothing more on his mind than sex with the two women so taking them to Tanner's Close, where Helen McDougall would have been waiting, was out of the question.

Con Burke had left for his street-sweeping job but his wife, displaying some fine Irish hospitality, made the three of them some breakfast and watched as they swilled copious amounts of whisky. Soon Mary had drunk herself unconscious so Burke turned his amorous intentions to her friend, Janet. Unfortunately, he had forgotten to tell her he was already spoken for, an omission soon remedied when Helen McDougall arrived looking for her man. She took one look at Burke with the drunken beauty and launched a tirade of verbal vitriol at them both. Burke halted the flow with a well-aimed glass, which sliced a bloody gash on Nelly's temple, before throwing her out of the room and slamming the door against her furious screeching. By this time, whatever ardour Janet may have been feeling had cooled and she wanted to leave so Burke – ever the gentleman – escorted her from the house, leaving Mary Paterson snoring softly behind them.

By the time he returned, Con's wife had alerted William Hare and Maggie Laird. The men swiftly realised that, in the body of the still unconscious Mary Paterson, they had an ideal opportunity for some trade so they ushered their respective wives out of the room, with Nell still breathing fire and venom. The shapely corpse of the young girl soon ended up on the anatomist's slab – much to the delight of the many doctors whose fascination with its beauty bordered on the necrophilic. An artist was even called to record it for posterity and the body itself was preserved in alcohol for some time.

Did Laird and McDougall know what was going to happen when they left the room? It is entirely probable. Their men had come into quite a bit of money lately and it could not all have been earned through renting rooms and repairing shoes. The men had hinted they were moonlighting as resurrectionists but, surely, their women knew them better than that. Maggie Laird had already assisted in luring one victim to her doom and had even, it seems, fetched a chest for the body to be placed in. And then there was McDougall's jealous rage to consider. Would she allow him to remain in a room, even with Hare, while an equally beautiful young girl lay insensate over the table?

However, Mary Paterson was no stranger in the city. She was a well-known streetwalker – even one of Knox's students recognised her – and, unlike the previous nonentities, her disappearance was noted. On top of this, there was also a witness – Janet Brown – who returned to the rooms in search of her friend. But, by this time, Mary was dead and her body was hidden behind a curtain. While Burke went out to find a tea chest to put her in before she was carted round to Surgeon's Square, Janet sipped whisky with Hare, Laird and a still-seething McDougall. She could have gone the way of her friend had her brothel-keeper not sent someone to fetch her.

Maggie and Helen also had a part to play in a double slaying – that of a woman from Glasgow and her deaf mute grandson. They helped get the old woman drunk and then sat at the fireside with the twelve-year-old boy while their menfolk committed murder in another room. What did they think was going to happen when Burke and Hare, with their faces flushed from their exertions and deeply lined in the dancing light of the flames, took the lad from them? And did they ask no questions when, come first light, neither grandmother nor grandson was anywhere to be seen? Did they ask no questions at all when the victims vanished? Or did they just help drink away the money earned from the sale of the corpses and prefer not to think about it?

But Maggie Laird continued to mistrust Helen McDougall until at one point, according to Burke, she suggested they do away with her. Burke, of course, refused but it was clear that the team was beginning to fragment. In June 1828, Burke and Helen left Edinburgh to visit her father in Falkirk. While they were away, Hare committed another murder, either a solo effort or in conjunction with his wife. Burke was displeased at this attempt at sole trading and, with Maggie Laird's homicidal thoughts towards his woman fresh in his mind, moved out of Tanner's Close and took a room nearby with a cousin.

Burke and Hare may no longer have been bosom buddies but their murdering ways continued. They had come too far together to stop – and, if a system ain't broke, don't fix it. The victims came fast and furious now. There was an ageing prostitute, followed by her daughter. Then Ann McDougall, a Falkirk woman who was a cousin of Nelly's former partner, had the misfortune to come visiting. But they made a mistake this time – one that could have proved fatal. Her body was actually seen by John Broggan, the husband of Burke's cousin. However, a few glasses of whisky and some pound notes ensured his silence. The money was supposed to pay Broggan's back rent but he made off with it, leaving Burke to foot the bill.

Here again, the question of Helen McDougall's complicity must be raised. Ann McDougall was a friend of Helen and, during her visit, she had apparently vanished without a word. What did she think had happened? Did she even care? Later, her actions were to prove that she knew exactly what her man had been up to all this time. But, before that, Maggie Laird took an active role in another murder.

'Daft' Jamie Wilson, like Mary Paterson, was well known on the streets of the Old Town as he limped about on his deformed bare feet. The eighteen-year-old was mentally retarded but he was well liked and wholly dependent on the charity of locals. While Burke was in a tavern enjoying his now customary early morning drink, he spotted Maggie Laird leading the lad towards Tanner's Close. Later the woman returned, asked him to buy her a drink and, while they sat together, she touched his foot with her own. Burke knew this was the signal that they had another pigeon for the plucking. Clearly, they had done this before. Later, Laird left Jamie in a room alone with Burke and Hare and a bottle of whisky. Just to make sure they were not disturbed, she locked the door behind her.

She knew what she was doing. She knew it when she took the boy into her home. She knew it when she gave Burke the signal. She knew it when she left the three of them alone in that bleak back room and locked the door.

But Jamie was too well known a victim. News of his disappearance spread quickly and reached the ears of Dr Knox while the body still lay on his examination table. There were no signs of foul play – the method of murder saw to that – but, nevertheless, he ordered that the body be anatomised quickly, with one assistant cutting off the head and deformed feet to avoid it being recognised.

Killing Jamie was a mistake but they had, once again, got away with it. However, time was running out for the fearsome foursome. They were about to go a victim too far. And this time they would all be involved.

It was sweet-talking William Burke who brought the woman, Mary Docherty, back to the room he shared with Helen McDougall. It was Halloween which was fitting considering the dark work that was to be done that night. He had come across the destitute

Irishwoman begging in a pub and had inveigled his way into her trust by suggesting they might be related. At that time, they were sharing the room with James Gray and his wife, Ann. Burke and Nelly would regret ever being tempted to sublet their space.

Burke told the Grays that he had arranged for them to have a bed at Tanner's Close with his good friends the Hares. Mrs Docherty was a relative, he explained, and it was his wish that she spend the night. Hare and Laird duly turned up to escort the Grays to their establishment but they returned to Burke's room shortly afterwards. Later, the four were seen drinking, singing and dancing with the woman who was to form part of their stock in trade.

The following day the Grays returned to find the Irishwoman gone. Helen McDougall told them Mrs Docherty had been 'using too much freedom with William [Burke]' and she had been forced to kick 'the damned bitch's backside out the door'. At one point Mrs Gray had settled herself down on the edge of the bed and Burke had snapped at her, 'Keep out of there, keep out of the straw.'

The Grays were bustled out of the room but later stole back in when Burke and McDougall had gone. Rooting around in the straw, they uncovered Mary Docherty's naked body, blood crusting around her mouth and nose. Shocked, they hurried from the room and came face to face with Helen McDougall on the stairs. Mr Gray challenged her over the dead body and she slumped to her knees and begged him not to say anything, offering him money for his silence. But the Grays were not like John Broggan, who had accepted cash to forget he'd seen the body of Ann McDougall. They rushed out into the street to fetch the police, only to find Maggie Laird. She tried to talk them into going back into the house to discuss the matter but the Grays, wisely, refused to go. They did, however, go to a nearby pub.

By the time the police were alerted and had stirred themselves to investigate the claims of foul murder, the body of Mrs Docherty had been folded into a tea chest – bought by Burke but collected by Maggie Laird – and whisked off to the waiting hands and scalpels of the doctors. But an examination of the bedding and straw revealed the dead woman's clothes and some blood. On questioning, Burke said the woman had left early that morning but McDougall said she had left the previous night – and she had spoken to her since. Presented with an obvious contradiction, the police took the couple into custody.

Further inquiries unearthed a local man who had carried the tea chest to Surgeon's Square. He knew there was a body inside because he himself had tucked away some hair that was hanging out. On arriving at Dr Knox's establishment, police found the corpse still in its makeshift coffin. Hare and his wife were arrested but denied ever having seen the dead woman. This was folly on their part because they knew that a number of people, including the Grays, had seen them all with Mrs Docherty while she was alive.

After being charged, Burke changed his story, inventing a mysterious hooded stranger carrying a large box who had come to have his shoes mended. While he was busy cobbling, Burke said that he had heard the rustle of straw behind him and, after the mystery man had left, he had found the body of the woman hidden beneath the bed. Later he tried a new tack. He admitted that the dead woman was Mrs Docherty, that she had been with them that night but that she had somehow suffocated herself while drunk. He and Hare had seized the opportunity to make some cash by selling the corpse to the anatomists. Hare, meanwhile, blamed another tenant, saying he had struck the woman. McDougall insisted she knew nothing of the murder, while no one knows what Maggie Laird was saying.

The authorities had a body. They had witnesses who placed the victim in the company of the Burkes and Hares on the night she died. Unfortunately, they had very little else. A post-mortem revealed that, although the woman had been suffocated, it was impossible to state with any certainty she was a victim of murder. What was needed was an eyewitness to the killing – and unfortunately the only people who knew what went on in that room were the accused foursome. Unless one or more of the alleged accomplices decided to confess or inform on the others, there was every chance they would all be freed on a not proven verdict. Perhaps a deal could be made. Perhaps one or more of them could be offered immunity in return for their freedom. Scottish justice is renowned for turning a blind eye to the misdeeds of witnesses testifying on the Crown's behalf. A conviction, any conviction, is better than nothing. And so the offer was made to William Hare and Maggie Laird. And they accepted.

With further information coming in regarding the disappearances of Mary Paterson and Jamie Wilson, that left only William Burke on three counts of murder – Daft Jamie, Mary Paterson and Mary Docherty. Helen McDougall was charged only in connection with Mary Docherty. In the end, thanks to protests from Burke's crack defence team – acting, as was the custom, free of charge – only Mary Docherty's death would trouble the court.

The trial began on the morning of Christmas Eve, 1828, and sat, without break, for a full twenty-four hours. There were fifty-five witnesses cited to appear. Dr Knox was listed but, amazingly, he was not called – fuelling conspiracy theories that the entire case was somehow designed to cover up the involvement of influential medical men and to protect the establishment of the day. However, the most important witnesses were undoubtedly William Hare and his wife, Maggie Laird.

Hare, of course, blamed Burke for just about everything, while being careful not to implicate himself too much. He was allowed to decline answers to certain questions that may have shown he was more involved in the murders than he claimed. Although Burke's defence tried to break this wall of silence, the prosecution defended Hare's stance. They were there to obtain a conviction not to unearth the truth.

Laird appeared holding her young child whose father was possibly Hare. The youngster was sick with whooping cough and she used it like a prop, tending to it while she thought about what she was saying. She did, however, make one slip of the tongue that may have passed unnoticed at the time but which has been seized on by writers since. She claimed that she and Helen McDougall had fled the room when Burke fell on Mrs Docherty. When she was asked what she thought had happened to the woman, she said she 'had a supposition that she had been murdered'. Then she added, 'I have seen such tricks before.'

She had seen such tricks before. Maggie Laird, a star prosecution witness, knew of previous murders. And she was getting away with it. None of the lawyers picked up on the remark. Perhaps their wits were dulled by the hours of continual evidence. Perhaps they caught it but chose to let it go. It would have suited the prosecution to do this because they had already agreed to try only the one murder. And the defence failed to follow it up because there would have been no benefit to their client to do so. Or perhaps neither side wanted the full extent of the West Port horrors to come out in a court of law.

The jury took just under an hour to reach their guilty verdict on William Burke. But it was only a majority verdict – two of the jurors remained unconvinced of his complete guilt. The press and populace at large were happy he had been convicted but felt the courts had not gone far enough. They felt that equally nefarious villains were escaping the noose – William Hare, Maggie Laird and Dr Robert Knox who, it was believed, must have known just how his two suppliers were gathering their merchandise.

The charge against Helen McDougall was found not proven. When he heard the verdict on his lover, Burke remarked, 'Nelly, you're out of the scrape.'

Much to the relief of the medical establishment and also to the prosecuting authorities, there was no need to try Burke on the other two charges – those of Mary Paterson and Jamie Wilson. After all, he could only hang once. The presiding judge, Lord Justice Clerk Boyle, stated that Burke had no chance of a pardon. He continued:

The only doubt I have in my mind in order to satisfy the violated laws of your country and the voice of public indignation is whether your body should not be exhibited in chains to bleach in the winds, to deter others from the commission of such offences but, taking into consideration the public eye would be offended by such a dismal spectacle, I am willing to accede to a more lenient execution of your sentence, that your body should be publicly dissected.

It was an ironic twist in the tale, considering the way Burke had made his most recent living. But the judge had another comment to make, opining that, if it was ever customary for the skeletons of murderers to be kept after dissection, then he hoped Burke's would be one 'in order that posterity may keep in remembrance of your atrocious crimes'.

The Edinburgh Tolbooth had been demolished in 1817 so Burke was taken first to Calton Jail and then, in preparation for his final public appearance, to the lock-up house in Libberton's Wynd. He made two confessions during this time, admitting sixteen murders but claiming William Hare had more to do with them than he had stated in court. He also removed any blame from his lover, Helen McDougall, and, to an extent, from Maggie Laird. However, there can be little doubt that both women knew exactly what was going on – if not at first, then certainly as the death tally rose. They had stood outside the room in Gibb's Close while their husbands finished off poor Mary Paterson and they had sat at the table drinking as her body cooled on a bed behind a curtain. Maggie Laird had helped lure Daft Jamie and others to their doom. Helen McDougall had remained silent when her ex-partner's cousin, Ann McDougall, disappeared. They had both waited with the deaf-mute Glasgow lad while the men slaughtered his grandmother and then they had allowed him to be led away to his own certain death. They had both been present when Burke and Hare plied poor Mrs Docherty with drink, although they had fled as the murder began. Helen had tried to buy the Grays' silence when they found the corpse of Ann McDougall and Maggie had attemp-

91

ted to calm them down. They had lied to the police over the night's events. Maggie Laird had admitted in court that 'she had seen such tricks before' after supposing Mrs Docherty had been murdered.

But, guilty or innocent, on Wednesday 28 January 1829, it was only Burke who paid the price for their collective misdeeds. The gallows itself was constructed in the Lawnmarket, not far from the lock-up house. The event was to be quite a spectacle. Signs were posted on windows on the tall buildings overlooking the execution site advertising an uninterrupted vantage point from which to witness the hanging. Despite fees being set as high as a guinea, there was a huge demand for places. Sir Walter Scott found himself such a window at 423 High Street to watch the show. The streets below were full of people – as many as 25,000, it has been estimated – and, as Burke was led on to the platform, a great wave of revulsion rose from their throats. This tide of hatred was not just aimed at the man on the scaffold but also towards the two men deemed by public indignation to be just as guilty – William Hare and Robert Knox. However, they had to be satisfied with just one hanging. Burke died easily, his body jerking minimally at the end of the drop. After the light-footed Irishman danced his last jig, the huge crowd celebrated with three loud cheers.

His body hung for an hour before it was taken down and transported to the dissecting rooms of Dr Alexander Monro. The butchery was to be a public event and, again, demand to view the event was great. The lecture theatre was filled to capacity and the usual angry crowd gathered outside. Police had to be called to keep order but, in the way that police often can, they only managed to make a bad situation worse. Anger turned to fury and fury turned to violence, with the mob trading blows with baton-wielding officers. While Burke's blood flowed in the lecture room, more blood was spilled in the streets and order was not restored until some arrangement could be made to allow as many people as possible to see Burke's corpse. Medical students were given priority to see the actual anatomising but, the following day, the public would be allowed to view the corpse lying on the slab. Again it is estimated that as many as 25,000 people filed past the sliced-up cadaver. The body was then flayed and the skeleton sent to Edinburgh University's anatomical museum for display. The skin was cut up into strips and sold as macabre keepsakes. One strip of skin, died blue, eventually came into the possession of Strathclyde Police's Black Museum at Pitt Street, Glasgow. Meanwhile, the rope that had been used to hang Burke was sold to a man for half a crown per inch.

During the dissection, it was revealed that Burke was suffering from testicular cancer. Had justice waited much longer to catch up with him, he would have cheated the hangman.

Perhaps Helen McDougall was in the Lawnmarket that Thursday to see her man die but probably not. Courtroom sketches had been well circulated and, after being released from prison, she had found her face too weel kent in the streets for her comfort. During an early excursion to buy liquor, she had been recognised and surrounded by angry townsfolk. The fifteen good men and true of the jury may not have been convinced of her guilt but these people were. Rough justice would almost certainly have been dispensed there and then had police officers not rescued the miserable woman and spirited her away. Later, disguised as a man, she was led from the police station and set free again. She thought it best to leave Edinburgh and return home to Falkirk but her welcome there was somewhat on the chilly side so she once again found herself back in Auld Reekie. She did not tarry there long but left Scotland altogether, winding up in Newcastle. There was talk that she emigrated to Australia but there is nothing concrete to support this.

Maggie Laird fared little better at the hands of the mob. She was given her liberation on Saturday 24 January 1829 but did not actually leave the jail until the following Monday when, like Helen McDougall, she was spotted in the streets. A dangerous crowd surrounded her in the High Street and would have done her some mischief had she not had her young child in her arms. The furious

93

people contented themselves with pelting her with snowballs although one gent did succeed in delivering a violent kick to her leg. Again police came to the rescue and steered her away from the jeering mob. She too realised that Edinburgh had grown too hot for her and, after a period spent wandering the country, she finally arrived in Glasgow with a view to hopping aboard a boat bound for Ireland. But, even in Glasgow, she was recognised and she had to be rescued by police officers there as well. Finally, she did book passage for the Emerald Isle but nothing more is known of her.

William Hare was kept locked up for a period. His promise of immunity from prosecution did not prevent the mother and sister of Jamie Wilson from attempting to raise a private prosecution. Despite a public subscription being raised to help meet the costs, the action failed. Six judges pondered the matter and rejected it by four votes to two. It was agreed that the Lord Advocate's decision to grant immunity from prosecution meant immunity from any prosecution. In their opinion, justice was best served by sticking to the original deal, while the good name of the Scottish legal system was best not besmirched by any further investigation. In any case, by the time their lordships made their decision, Burke, who would necessarily have been an important witness, was dead.

And so William Hare was set free. The multiple murderer had assisted Scottish justice and that was that. It may have been a necessary evil to ensure that at least one person was punished for the horrors but, even today, almost 200 years later, it leaves a bad taste in the mouth. In February, Hare boarded a coach bound for England and, apart from a stopover in Dumfries, where he experienced the same kind of treatment as had already been meted out to his female accomplices, little definite is known about what he did next. Some say he wound up in London, begging in the streets. Others say he was recognised by workmen and blinded with quicklime. Yet others say he was lynched in Dublin or that he met the same fate in New York. Another version has him making his way back to Ireland where he was reunited with Maggie Laird.

But no one knows for sure. He, Maggie and Helen became shadows on the pages of history.

It is worth noting that, although William Hare avoided the drop, another Hare, a man reputed to be his nephew, did fulfill a date with the hangman. On 24 October 1851, Archibald Hare was hanged in Glasgow for stabbing a man in Blantyre. Like his alleged uncle, this Hare was described as being 'of repulsive and dogged aspect'. His drop was too short and he spun on the rope trying desperately to relieve the pressure on his neck with his hands. The hangman pulled down on his legs until he died.

Despite the best efforts of the establishment to protect him, Dr Robert Knox's medical career was more or less ruined – at least in Edinburgh. Angry townspeople thirsted for his blood and, if they could not hang him in earnest, they would hang him in effigy. His house was attacked and stoned, as was his anatomy theatre in Surgeon's Square. An inquiry was held but in the Scottish way – in private and in secret. By clearing Knox of any knowledge in regard to the murders, its findings failed to satisfy the public's expectations. Although many of his students still held him in high regard, his classes began to shrink. Shunned by friends and colleagues and with his professional abilities called into question, he left Edinburgh in 1840 and died in Hackney in 1862.

Revulsion over this case and others led to the review of the system of providing corpses to medical science. In 1832, MP Henry Warburton's bill to regulate the supply of bodies and make grave-robbing a felony was passed. With the stroke of a pen, the government had finally seen sense and brought this particular skin trade to an end.

But there is another character, albeit a bit player, in this drama whose fate is worth mentioning – John Broggan, the man who had accepted money to keep quiet about seeing the body of Ann McDougall in Burke and McDougall's house. He had made off with the money and, in July 1829, was arrested in Glasgow for attempting to murder a man with laudanum.

The appearance of this drug in connection with the Burke and

Hare case is interesting. For, while the furore over the West Port murders continued to rage in the early part of 1829, another pair of serial killers was operating. And their favoured method of murder was this opium-based narcotic.

Blackfriars Monastery is long gone but the site of James I's assassination is marked in Perth by this commemorative plaque (left).

There is little left of Dunbar Castle now but Mary, Queen of Scots would have known it well. She fled here with Darnley following the murder of her secretary, David Rizzio. It was here that she and Bothwell became lovers and they came here again after her nobles had rebelled against her.

Mary, Queen of Scots' house in Jedburgh. Here she hovered close to death after falling into a marsh during a helter-skelter ride across the moors to visit the wounded Earl of Bothwell at Hermitage Castle. Her husband, Lord Darnley, was murdered not long after this event.

Edinburgh from the Fife coast (above). Accused murderess Katharine Nairn would have had a view similar to this as she was ferried across the Forth to the city for trial. A crowd, awaiting her arrival at Leith, was incensed because she was laughing and joking with the ferrymen. The city, of course, has been host to many a dark deed and grisly execution – from Queen Joan's revenge on her husband's assassins to Jessie King's series of child murders. Arthur's Seat is on the left and the castle on the right.

Women who broke Kirk law could be put in the 'jougs' and held up to ridicule by fellow parishioners. This particular example can still be found on the wall of Fenwick Church, Ayrshire.

Edinburgh's Tolbooth, the infamous Heart of Midlothian, which housed many a felon and was the scene of Katharine Nairn's daring jailbreak. The platform, visible at the left-hand side, was used as a gallows.

The Scottish Maiden, the beheading device that claimed the life of Jean Livingston and many others. The original design may have been brought to Scotland from Halifax by Regent Morton who ironically later lost his head under its blade.

Contemporary reports stated that Helen MacDougall, wife of William Burke, possessed a faded beauty but there's little evidence of it in this print.

As the scourge of bodysnatching grew, relatives attempted to protect their dead loved ones with devices such as this heavy metal mortsafe (above), which was clamped over the grave to prevent access. But it did not stop Jean Waldie and Helen Torrence from snatching the Dallas boy while he was still alive. And nor did it prevent Burke and Hare, with their respective wives' connivance and aid, from murdering people to keep Edinburgh's surgeons supplied with cadavers. This mortsafe can be found in Ayr's New Kirkyard.

HARE'S WIFE AND CHILD.
TAKEN FROM A SKETCH FURNISHED BY ONE OF THE JURY.

Maggie Laird, the wife of murderer William Hare, sketched as she gave her evidence against William Burke and Helen MacDougall.

A contemporary print showing the execution of William Burke on Edinburgh's Lawnmarket. Around 20,000 people attended the event with the well-to-do renting space at the windows overlooking the gallows.

The new jail on Edinburgh's Calton Hill replaced the old Tolbooth. William Burke was kept here for a time and Jessie King was executed behind these walls.

Glasgow's Duke Street Prison, which no longer exists but stood near to the Cathedral. Susan Newell was hanged here and Jeannie Donald served her prison term behind these walls.

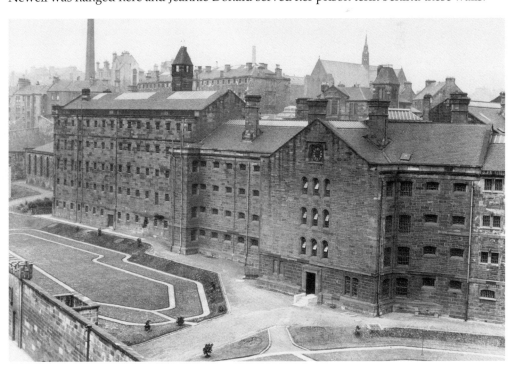

Sheila Garvie in later years.

7

TIPPING THE DOCTOR

Catherine Stuart, 1828

The nightmare was always the same. She awoke to find him watching her from the walls of the room. No matter which way she turned, his pallid face gleamed in the dark, his accusing eyes burning into her soul. Even when she closed her eyes, she still saw the hellish vision. Liquor could not wash it from her mind nor could tobacco burn it from her conscience. Night after night, he visited her, torturing her, reminding her of her crime, of the life she had helped take.

Her partner was of stronger mettle and saw no such spectres in the night but he was fearful his wife's distemper would prove their undoing. He tried to calm her, to reassure her, but still she was tormented by the nocturnal terrors. So they suffered and they fretted and the woman, at least temporarily, regretted the course their life had taken.

But it did not stop them from killing again.

Catherine Wright met John Stuart in Dumfries in 1827 and he probably led her astray. He was already an experienced thief but not yet a murderer. When he did take that step, however, his wife would be by his side to administer the poison that would claim up to eleven lives.

Stuart's real name was Bradfoot and his poor Irish parents rented a small farm in Galloway. However, the farm failed, either through misfortune or their own mismanagement, so they sent their son to Glenluce to work. He worked as a blacksmith for a man who was described as 'pious, benevolent and good-hearted'. His employer found his young charge to be 'industrious, sober and frugal'. But this was not destined to last. It was the love of a woman that caused the change in young John Bradfoot's personality.

In 1823, at the age of twenty, he married a young girl from a respectable local family. The girl's family disapproved of the match, believing their daughter had married beneath her, and made their feelings more than evident every single day. At first, young John tried to ignore their jibes and snide remarks but then something snapped and he knew he had to get away. He had no way of knowing that, by joining the Marines, he was going to affect not only his life adversely but also that of his delicate young wife, who was not coping well with her family's rejection. She did not take readily to life as a soldier's wife and, soon after arriving at Chatham Barracks, she took ill and died. Bradfoot obtained a pass to go back to Scotland with their only child but he failed to return.

Now a deserter, Bradfoot underwent the personality change that was to lead him to theft, murder and ultimately the gibbet. He was a tortured soul with low self-esteem and this confusion of the mind led his old friends to shun him. From there it was but a short step to fall into the company of 'idle and unprincipled profligates'. He moved around the country, stealing what he could, although he was too fearful to attempt anything as daring as housebreaking or highway robbery. According to a report on the case in *The Scotsman*, 'sheep stealing was his boldest adventure' although he did prove himself to be 'a pretty dexterous pickpocket', targeting county fairs. He also gambled extensively and learned the delicate art of cheating in order to reduce the possibility of losing any of his ill-gotten gains. He did, however, at one point manage to stage a break-out from Stranraer Jail. Later, while on remand for murder, he would plot a more adventurous and bloody escape from Edinburgh's Calton Jail.

For two years, he ran with a band of coiners and passers of forged bank-notes from whom he learned some brand new skills. He was smart enough to realise that he could not escape the interest of the law forever and that the perils of being caught increased along with the number of accomplices a man had. There is no such thing as honour among thieves, he knew, and it was certain that, if any of his partners-in-crime were caught, he would inform on the others faster than a man could be turned off the gallows.

So, using his new-found skills, he went into business for himself, operating first in the Borders then taking up residence in a small room in Dumfries. He proved adept at forgery, devising his own moulds and dyes, but he also took odd jobs, including work as a blacksmith, to explain the cash he often had to spend.

It was around this time that he met the young girl who was to be his second wife. Born in Glasgow but raised in Dumfries, Catherine Wright was aged around twenty and was bowled over by Bradfoot – or Stuart, as he was now calling himself – who could be a charming fellow when he wasn't blind drunk. By all accounts, they were very much in love and were married, fittingly for a man who worked in a smithy, over the anvil in Gretna. Together they began a two-year-long crime spree. He showed her some of the tricks of his new trade and they ran up a wad of counterfeit cash. They then embarked on a tour of Scotland, Northern England and Ireland to convert the forged notes into coin of the realm. Unfortunately, they seemed incapable of hanging on to their ill-gotten gains, both having a weakness for strong drink and debauchery.

Stuart was growing tired of coining. He needed a new outlet for his criminal talents and apparently he found it during one of his trips away from Dumfries. While travelling between Edinburgh and Biggar, he met an old acquaintance, who was then preparing to rob a genteel family while they were 'wrapped in profound repose'. The old partner-in-crime told him this was to be his last such job for he had discovered a much more lucrative way to make a living. He planned to use drugs, specifically laudanum, to render victims senseless so they could be plundered at leisure. The idea appealed to Stuart and he returned to Dumfries to outline the new trade to his wife. She agreed and they set off immediately for Glasgow.

Laudanum really was the opium of the masses. At the time it

was used extensively among the poorer classes as a medicine and a means of dulling the harsh realities of their life. Stuart called their method of robbery 'tipping the Doctor'. The problem was that neither of them had any experience of administering such a sleeping draught so Stuart took the dangerous step of experimenting on himself first by taking different doses. They did enjoy some success in Glasgow but had the sense to realise that lingering too long in one place left them open to having their collars felt.

Then they killed their first victim.

They befriended a quiet, good man with few friends. Catherine poured him some liquor, laced with the laudanum, while her husband exuded bonhomie. The little man, the poisoned drink in his hand, was just grateful that he had at last found good company in which to spend a few hours. He thanked his hosts for being such kind people and then drank deeply. His new-found friends then robbed him blind and left him to die.

This was the man in Catherine's nightmares. And they would not let her rest. Although concerned that her discomfort would bring the law down on them, her husband refused to leave her and determined to help pull her through. He did a good job for she managed to keep her niggling conscience under control enough to allow them to pursue fresh victims. 'The Doctor' was, once again, back in business.

According to one report, a man was killed in full view of the customers in a tavern in Glasgow's Bridgegate. The Doctor had duly done his job and, while the patient was slumped senseless, they rifled his pockets and relieved him of 30 shillings. They told the publican that the man was their brother and that they would leave him there to sleep it off while they went off to find lodgings. Naturally, they never returned. Another victim was said to be a drover in Ireland, who was drugged and robbed of the 20 or 30 sovereigns he had hidden in the tail of his coat.

No one knows exactly how many men tasted the Doctor's medicine and awoke to find themselves somewhat ill and considerably poorer. It was believed the Stuarts killed three men during this time although, according to the press reports, Stuart later confessed to eleven murders in total. The pair's downfall, though, was the robbery and murder of a Hebridean businessman in December 1828.

When farmer, merchant and father of four, Robert Lamont, left his home on the remote isle of Ulva with his cousin John on his annual trip to Glasgow to buy tea, sugar and tobacco, he was in fine health and had in his possession a black leather pocket book containing £10 in bank notes, a £2 note from the Leith Bank and 7 guineas in bankers' notes, as well as some silver coins in a black silk purse.

On 15 December at Lochgilphead, the fifty-year-old boarded the Royal Mail packet steamer, the *Toward Castle*, travelling to Glasgow from Inveraray. It was while in the steerage compartment, where drinks were sold, that he fell in with what he called 'fine company'. Unfortunately for him that fine company included John and Catherine Stuart, who were already drinking with a Mrs Catherine McPhail and her granddaughter. Mrs McPhail was a hawker and sometime smuggler, who was raging over the fact that a customs officer had impounded two kegs of whisky from her baggage. The nice young Mrs Stuart was trying to cheer her up with a glass of porter when Robert Lamont joined them. He instantly called for another bottle but was informed there was none left. They would have to make do with gills of whisky and strong ale, which was taken into the charge of Mrs Stuart.

For some reason, they were all forced to drink from the same glass and, when it came time for a refill, John Stuart distracted everybody's attention while his black-gloved wife poured. John Lamont, though, refused little more than a few sips, finding the ale somewhat bitter. Mrs McPhail, who admitted she was no stranger to strong liquor, also declined to sup much from the bottle, despite Mrs Stuart's sharp order, 'Damn you – drink it all!' The woman was resolute and the glass passed to Robert Lamont.

However, when it was Mr Stuart's turn, the company was treated to a minor domestic dispute. As he raised the glass to his lips, his wife angrily slapped it from his grip and damned him for a blackguard, telling him he must not get himself drunk. She then refilled the glass from her bottle and handed it to Robert Lamont. He was about to decline but she insisted, saying, 'It is your drink and you must drink it.'

John Lamont decided he'd had enough of the stuffy but highly charged atmosphere below decks and went topside for some air, leaving his cousin with the Stuarts. On deck, he felt extremely ill, being racked by 'a severe griping of the bowels'. From then on, he vomited every half-hour. When the vessel reached Paisley Water, he went back down to fetch Robert to prepare for their arrival in Glasgow. He found his cousin alone 'and in a fit of insensibility', his head slumped between his knees and unable to either speak or move. In John Lamont's words, the man's 'limbs refused to perform their office'. Knowing that copious amounts of beer had been flowing, John at first presumed Robert Lamont was drunk but he also suspected that he had been robbed. A swift check of his pockets proved this to be correct. The black leather wallet lay on the floor beneath his feet but it was empty. Gone also was the silk purse.

When told of this, William Stewart, master of the *Toward Castle*, was not surprised. He had been involved in an earlier encounter with the Stuarts, soon after they had come on board at Inveraray. When asked for the money for their fare, they had said they were near penniless, having left all their belongings on the ferry bound for Belfast. The ferry had docked at Inveraray because of poor weather and had then sailed without them earlier that day. On the *Toward Castle*, they had paid their passage as far as Greenock but, later, were in sufficient funds to cough up more cash to take them all the way to Glasgow. Captain Stewart recalled they were both somewhat the worse for drink.

After discovering the robbery, John Lamont reported it to the captain who found Mrs Stuart alone below decks. She explained her husband was in the water closet and, when the man came out, the captain asked him about their erstwhile drinking companion. Stuart said the man had got so drunk they had been forced to leave him. When Stuart was asked how much cash he had on him, he claimed it was about £20, despite having earlier pleaded poverty. He agreed to a search and, sure enough, was found to have £19 7s. He was also found to have a black silk purse similar to the one previously carried by Robert Lamont. The purse itself was distinctive, as the man's daughter had sewn it herself. Meanwhile, a small square bottle smelling strongly of laudanum was found in the water closet John Stuart had so recently vacated.

By this time, the boat had berthed at Glasgow's Broomielaw and three doctors were called. They immediately suspected Robert Lamont had been poisoned and, when told, a weak and pale John Lamont said, 'If he was poisoned, then I have had a glass of it.' Mrs McPhail was also vomiting copiously and it was clear they had a touch of whatever ailed the still insensate farmer. They were luckier than he was to be, though, for, despite the medical treatment, Robert Lamont died at 5.30 a.m. the following morning.

There was little mystery as to the cause of death. Doctors had pumped his stomach when they boarded and found that the contents smelt strongly of laudanum. Meanwhile, his vomit was gathered into a glass jar and given to the police. The doctors believed the symptoms exhibited by the dead man were consistent with laudanum poisoning and of such a considerable dose that its odour could be detected over the stench of the beer.

In Glasgow, William Davie, the Assistant Town Clerk, questioned both John Lamont and Mrs McPhail. He called for a bottle of strong ale, tipped a penny's worth of laudanum into it and asked them both to take a sip. They promptly confirmed that it tasted similar to the ale served by Mrs Stuart on the boat.

The Stuarts had already been arrested and taken away for questioning. It was clear there was sufficient evidence to charge the husband and wife team of murder and send them for trial in July 1829. John Stuart, however, was not prepared simply to sit in a cell and wait for the machinery of justice to stretch his neck. He planned a daring escape with another eight men, described at the time as 'stout and desperate ruffians'. The plan was to murder a warder, take his keys, then rampage through the prison before killing the depute governor. This daring bid for freedom was set to take place the day before Stuart's trial. An alternative plan was also hatched. This involved the use of whatever weapons they could gather – including a wooden seat they had prised from its bolts on the floor and some metal spikes sawed from railings and sharpened into daggers – to fight their way out, killing anyone who got in their way.

But someone talked, as someone often does, and their schemes were uncovered. The spikes were found hidden in Stuart's cell and, when challenged, he said, 'It was no more than anyone else would have done.'

The trial began with some legal jiggery-pokery concerning the indictment, which stated that, on 15 December 1828, they 'did both, and each or one or other of them, go on board the *Toward Castle* steamship plying on the River and Firth of Clyde from Inveraray to Glasgow and, when the said steamship was between Tarbert and Glasgow, they did wilfully, wickedly and feloniously administer to Robert Lamont, a passenger, a quantity of laudanum, being a deadly poison'. Lamont, it said, lingered in a state of utter insensibility until the morning of 16 December 1828, when he died.

The defence contended that the indictment was incompetent because it did not state how the deadly poison was actually administered and pointed out that it might have been for 'laudable purposes'. In other words, the Stuarts – if they had, indeed, slipped him the alleged Mickey – might have done so for the good of his health and with his consent. If that was the case, it was gamely argued, they should not be charged with the capital crime of murder but with the less serious crime of culpable homicide – or manslaughter, as it is known outwith Scotland. Also, it was pointed out that the indictment did not specify exactly where death oc-curred. It could have been anywhere between Lochgilphead and

Glasgow. For all the court knew, it could have been in England. The medical treatment the man received was also raised. Mrs Stuart's advocate demanded to know if Mr Lamont's stomach had been pumped and if every precaution had been taken to lengthen or protect his life.

All this was just a brave attempt to stave off the inevitable. It was argued that the indictment did not need to state where the man actually died and the attempts made to revive him would soon be made clear. As for the possibility that the drug had been administered for altruistic reasons, the subsequent robbery showed that this was not the case. The Lord Advocate dealt with each objection and presented arguments that convinced the bench to deny the defence's objections. Meanwhile, the witnesses were paraded before the fifteen good men and true of the jury.

According to the prosecution, Stuart was apt to boast about his crimes. Certainly, even today, criminals can establish their place in the prison pecking order by crowing to fellow convicts over the charges lodged against them. However, it is unlikely that quite so many of them confess to complete strangers as the prosecuting authorities claim. In this case, one Malcolm Logan, who was doing six months for handling stolen goods, told the court that Stuart had said that his wife kept the poison in the square bottle and that it was she who had dropped the poison into the ale. After they had drugged and robbed Mr Lamont, Stuart then took the bottle and flushed what was left of the laudanum down the water closet. However, no amount of rinsing out could wash away the strong smell from the bottle itself.

For the first time, the court heard that Stuart called laudanum 'the Doctor'.

'He said that by "giving the Doctor",' said Logan, 'he meant that he would give it to any person who had money about them and he would set them asleep and he would rob them.'

Of course, the authorities already knew all of this and it is not beyond the realms of possibility that, to strengthen their case, the prosecution had recruited Logan. There was a suggestion that he too had killed a man with a dose of the drug, which Logan, of course, denied. But, apparently, he had argued with Stuart in jail and threatened that 'he would see him hanging'. However, another prisoner, Archibald Anderson, corroborated Logan's story and a guard at Calton Jail testified that Stuart had asked him if anything he'd said to other prisoners could be used against him. According to the guard, Stuart told him he had been 'very foolhardy in speaking his mind' and that, if Logan and Anderson talked and their evidence was heard, he would be done for.

But, even without their evidence, the Stuarts were done for. The incriminating factors were: they had been drinking with Lamont; the beer served by Mrs Stuart tasted vile; a later test had showed that ale spiked with laudanum tasted similar; Lamont had an overdose of laudanum in his system; Stuart was found with money on him that could have come from Lamont's wallet; he was also found with the distinctive silk purse identified by Lamont's daughter as being the one she had made for her father; the small square bottle that stank of laudanum was found in the water closet that Stuart had just vacated.

The Lord Advocate said the deadly duo had been 'charged with murder and murder committed under circumstances of the most atrocious and most aggrievable nature'. Despite defence objections to the contrary, Lord Gillies, one of the three judges, believed it was clear that murder had been committed. He conceded it was possible that the deceased had taken the laudanum himself but he could not have robbed himself. In his opinion, the female accused 'cut by far the most conspicuous figure' in this murder. It was she who had brought the ale containing the poison but she had not drunk it nor had she allowed her husband to drink it.

Of course, the case was viewed as a warning to the lower and middle classes of the dangers not just of laudanum but also of the demon drink. Men, it was said, were exposed to such dangers 'by their passion for intoxicating liquors'.

Unsurprisingly, at the end of the twelve-hour trial the jury was out for only a few minutes. They returned with a unanimous verdict of guilty on both of the accused. On passing sentence, Lord Pitmilly said, 'all that remained for the court was a duty of a most distressing and painful nature.' Because of their acts, 'an innocent man had been bereaved of life and for his murder they must now atone to the outraged laws of the country.' He went on to say it was 'a crime of the most novel, most dangerous, most subtle and most daring nature'.

Settling the black cap on his head, he got down to his distressing and painful duty, declaring they were to be taken to the jail and there fed on bread and water under the terms of the 1752 Act for Preventing the Horrid Crime of Murder. Then, on 19 August, they were to be hanged at the common place of execution in the Lawnmarket in Edinburgh and their bodies delivered to Dr Alexander Monro, Professor of Anatomy at the university, in order to be publicly dissected and anatomised. The judge urged the prisoners to 'turn all their thoughts to the important concerns of another world and avail themselves of the attendance of pious people'.

At 8 p.m. on the night before their execution, the Stuarts were taken from their respective cells in Edinburgh's Calton Jail and moved to their new, if temporary, lodgings in the Libberton's Wynd lock-up house. Reunited in the same room for their final night, Mrs Stuart rushed into her husband's arms and he held her as well as he could, given that he was heavily chained. Those pious people, of whose services the judge had urged them to avail themselves, attended them. However, as the *Edinburgh Weekly Chronicle* reported, they did not seem to be sensible 'to the truths of religion, or to the probability of their proceeding directly from the hangman to a place of everlasting bliss'.

The pair had, though, expressed regrets over their crimes and Stuart intimated that they were responsible for a number of other deaths as well. His wife wept continually through the night and, when she was asked by one of the ministers who was attempting to tend to her spiritual wellbeing if it was the fear of death that tormented her, she replied, 'Oh yes, yes, yes, it is the fear of death.'

Murderers they may have been but, during this last night together, it was made obvious that there was deep feeling between the couple – which, as one newspaper reported, 'increased in strength as they approached the final hour'. John Stuart tried to comfort his wife throughout, at one point attempting to hush her tears by saying that they were now 'only in the hands of the Almighty'. This thought failed to bolster her spirits and her weeping continued.

Naturally, the knowledge of what was to happen the following morning murdered any thoughts of sleep and guards heard them whispering throughout the night. Meanwhile, outside, heavy rain beat a solemn tattoo on the walls and windows. At 5 a.m. the following morning, a minister returned and prayed with them for two hours. Finally, word was received that they were to prepare themselves for their final walk. They were allowed to change into fresh clothes – decent black ones, it was noted, courtesy of the prison governor.

As they waited for the appointed hour, Stuart asked for a cup of tea to be brought to his wife and together they listened to further religious exhortations. Mrs Stuart asked for a pipe and filled it with her own tobacco, which she lit from the fire. She puffed away studiously while the ministers continued to appeal to their spiritual nature, tears still glistening in her eyes and on her cheeks.

Then their time came. The executioner wanted to place the hood over their heads before they ascended to the platform but Mrs Stuart shook her head saying, 'No, no – you will surely allow us as much not to do that.' The hangman put the hoods aside, pinioned his two charges and then led them to where the gallows had been erected.

The rain showers of the previous night had, by this time, turned into a torrent but this did not prevent a huge crowd of people from showing up to see them hang. Over 10,000 people huddled in the downpour, watching the notorious murderers being taken to the platform – Stuart walking with a steady gait. When they were positioned under the two nooses, a murmur ran through the crowd.

As the ropes were placed around their necks, John Stuart trembled, his first real sign of any emotion, and lifted his eyes to the skies. His wife, though, had apparently found her composure and stood, as one observer put it, 'like marble'.

Stuart managed to stretch out one hand far enough for his wife to grip it and they murmured what could have been prayers. Then the hangman released the trapdoor and they fell together. Stuart died instantly, it seems, but his wife took longer, jerking and straining at the rope and her legs twitching. Her face, visible because she had opted not to wear a hood, was hideously contorted. The crowd watched this horrid spectacle for a few minutes before her body stilled and she once again joined her husband.

It would not be the last time Scottish courts would hear of poison.

8

LIFE AND DEATH
ON THE FARM

Christina Gilmour, 1842-3

Christina Cochran's father wanted the best for his daughter. Although far from penurious – his family were respected cheese-makers with a long-established farm at South Grange in Dunlop, part of Ayrshire's rich dairy land – this was 1842 and, being the head of a Victorian household, Alexander Cochran wanted his eldest lass to be comfortable. The problem was that Christina, or Kirsty, had fallen in love with the son of a neighbouring farmer. John Anderson was older than her by ten years but they had known each other since childhood. However, he was proving somewhat hesitant in plighting his troth, popping the question or taking the plunge. Like Alexander Cochran, Anderson was also a man of his times and he was unwilling to plight, pop or plunge without first being sure he could support a wife and, hopefully, a family.

But Christina loved him and wanted to marry him so she was willing to wait. Her father, though, had other ideas. Kirsty was now twenty-four and not getting any younger. All her life she had been trained to be a wife, even being sent off to Paisley for dressmaking lessons. It was time she was married – and married well.

Enter another John – Gilmour of that ilk. He was from successful farming stock and had his own land at Town of Inchinnan farm in Renfrewshire. He met Christina and immediately fell for her, for she was a bright and pretty lass, even though she had a slightly deformed right arm. In old Alexander's eyes, John Gilmour was a fitting match.

Naturally, Kirsty was not enthusiastic at the prospect of the union. Although he continued to show little sign of calling the bans, her heart was still set on John Anderson. Gilmour, meanwhile, was getting desperate and threatened suicide when the object of his affections remained cool. There was a lot of restrained passion going about in those days and suitors were prone to making such grand gestures. However, it is open to question whether a Central Scotland farmer, even one of the gentleman variety, would make such a threat unless he was suffering from some kind of mental illness.

Finally, the young woman put her cards on the table regarding John Anderson. She told him about the other John and of his offers of marriage, no doubt hoping Anderson would sweep her off to the matrimonial bed. But there was no such sweeping in her immediate future, for John Anderson did what he thought was the decent thing and gave up any claim he had on Kirsty's hand.

And so, on 29 November 1842, an unwilling, even despondent, Kirsty Cochran became Christina Gilmour and went off to live on her new husband's farm, taking family servant Mary Paterson with her. She did not love her husband. There was no conjugal bliss – she spent their wedding night in a chair by the fire. Gilmour took this treatment stoically, little knowing that, in six weeks, he would be dead of apparent arsenic poisoning.

John Gilmour took ill for the first time on Thursday 29 December 1842. He was vomiting violently, his face and eyes were swollen, he was in tremendous pain and these symptoms persisted for seventeen days until, on 11 January 1843, he died – and the rumours began. His wife had tended to him throughout his illness, said the whisperers. She had personally prepared every bit of food and drink. Perhaps she had poisoned him.

The suggestions of foul murder continued to circulate long after the man's funeral. Servants spoke of mysterious purchases of arsenic for and by Mrs Gilmour. They whispered darkly of her indifference to her husband during their short marriage. Her love of John Anderson was also a motivating factor, they said.

Finally, by April, the words from those wagging tongues reached official ears and noses began to twitch. Superintendent George McKay of the Renfrewshire Rural Police Force was sent to sniff around. He smelled something rotten and an application was made for an exhumation order. This was granted on 21 April – along with a warrant to arrest Christina Gilmour.

However, by that time, she had fled the country. Her father had heard the gossip, was naturally concerned for his daughter's wellbeing and had convinced her that it would be best if she made herself scarce. And so, one dark April night, the flight of Christina Gilmour began. It would end four months later in a courtroom on another continent.

When she left her father's farm, she had no idea where she was being taken. Her brother, Robert, had apparently made all the arrangements but, as he was never called as a witness in the subsequent trial, this point was never firmly established. Her companion was a man she did not know and he, in turn, left her in the charge of a second stranger, who conveyed her by gig (a two-wheeled one-horse buggy) to a man named Simpson who was to accompany her to Liverpool by rail. From there, she learned they would take a ship to America.

They arrived in Liverpool, booked their passage on a ship named the *Excel* under the names of Mr and Mrs John Spiers – the name 'John' seems to have haunted the woman – and set sail for what Christina's family hoped would be the land of the free. But she could not shake John Anderson from her mind and wrote him one last letter, telling him of her flight and complaining that Simpson was proving far from a gentleman. It seemed that he was taking the concept of man and wife somewhat further than a ruse to avoid detection.

She also claimed to have turned to the ship's captain for protection from her companion's sexual overtures but this seems unlikely as the two of them were supposed to be married and no one would have come between a married couple in those days.

Meanwhile, the huge mortsafe – a holdover from the days of the resurrection men – had been hoisted from John Gilmour's grave in Dunlop kirkyard and the body disinterred. Although it was badly decomposed and the face was unrecognisable, undertakers officially identified the corpse as that of Gilmour and then delivered it into the waiting hands and scalpels of doctors to allow them to examine the necessary organs. Sure enough, they found traces of arsenic.

Superintendent McKay, now with the scent of murder strong in his nostrils, proved to be something of a bloodhound and traced the fleeing Christina's movements to Liverpool. A new warrant was obtained and the seemingly unstoppable Scottish policeman booked passage on a faster vessel, arriving in New York three weeks ahead of his quarry. When her boat finally docked, the dogged detective, intent on making his arrest, was among the first to go on board. The ungentlemanly Mr Simpson, however, managed to escape into the teeming streets of New York and subsequent obscurity.

But Christina Gilmour was not ready to go quietly. The Treaty of Washington, an extradition agreement between the US and Great Britain, had been formalised in August the previous year and her New York lawyer was determined to fight her case all the way. Under the terms of the treaty, a person charged with murder in either country could only be sent back home if evidence of criminality were proved. That meant that there had to be a hearing before the US Commissioner, during which Christina's American lawyer argued that Mrs Gilmour was insane. To back this up, a team of doctors was brought in to study her but, although she sat on the floor, spoke gibberish and even cut herself, they formed the opinion that she was faking. Undeterred, the lawyer battled on, objecting to the evidence produced by Superintendent McKay, claiming the extradition treaty was invalid and even appealing to US President John Tyler. None of this was successful and, in

August 1843, Christina Gilmour was brought back to Scotland to face trial for her husband's murder.

But not everyone was convinced of her guilt. On Thursday 11 January 1844 – a year to the day after her husband died – she travelled by train from her jail cell in Paisley to Edinburgh. A report in the *Glasgow Courier* states:

> This unfortunate woman, to stand trial on Friday first before the High Court of Justiciars for the alleged poisoning of her husband, passed through Glasgow on her way to Edinburgh per railway.
>
> She was plainly but neatly attired and accompanied by the Matron of Paisley Prison and two officers.
>
> Mrs Gilmour paid for her own railway ticket, seemed quite cool and collected, and walked through the station house as if unaccompanied by no other person.
>
> She had about her none of that dejection or tremours which affects great criminals and is . . . rather a good-looking woman.

The trial excited great interest and spectators travelled from as far away as Ayrshire and Renfrewshire – no mean distance in those days. A contemporary record said that the 'circumstances of the case gave it an appeal to the public that had been unparalleled for several years. The doors of the courthouse were crowded with people from the early hours of the morning . . .' In fact, such was the crush of people eager to witness what promised to be a sensational trial that resourceful doorkeepers at the High Court saw a way of making some easy money and actually charged admission to the public gallery. On the second day of the trial, the Lord Justice-Clerk, Lord Moncrieff, one of the judges, heard about this spontaneous explosion of free enterprise and confessed to being 'astonished'. He pointed out that this practice was not only 'reprehensible' but also 'decidedly illegal' and urged anyone who had been forced to pay for a seat in the court to come forward and give evidence against the offending doorkeepers.

The trial lasted only two days – it may have taken them a year to bring the woman to court but they certainly weren't going to waste any time in having the matter resolved, at least in the eyes of the law. Christina Gilmour, dressed completely in black and wearing a plain gold wedding ring, listened to the evidence against her. She displayed no emotion during the testimony of prosecution witnesses, appearing indifferent – 'if not with apathy', as one reporter commented – to the legal battle raging around her.

The long and rambling indictment for murder claimed that Christina Gilmour did

> wickedly, maliciously and feloniously. . . cause to be taken by the said John Gilmour, in some article or articles of food or drink, or in some other manner to the prosecutors unknown, several or one or more quantities of arsenic, or other poisons . . . and the said John Gilmour . . . did immediately or soon after . . . become seriously ill and died suffering under violent and increased illness and did linger in great pain until the 11th day of January 1843 when he died . . . and was thus murdered by you, the said Christina Cochran, or Gilmour; and you . . . being conscious of your guilt in the premises, did abscond and flee from justice . . .

When asked, at the end of the somewhat wordy indictment, how she pleaded, the accused said in a calm, clear voice, 'Not Guilty, My Lord.' They were the only words she would utter throughout the two days for, at the time, accused people could not speak in their own defence.

And so the evidence began. Servants and friends of the deceased told the jury of fifteen men that Christina was in the habit of making tea for her husband and herself and prepared all the food. The jury was told she gave Mary Paterson tuppence to buy a bag of arsenic, to be used, she claimed, to poison rats. Curiously, she instructed the girl to find a boy and get him to buy the arsenic for her. Was this a bid to cover her tracks? Did she intend to murder her husband? However, Mary Paterson did not follow her mistress's instructions and she bought the arsenic herself – even providing

115

the druggist with Christina's name for the record he was bound by law to keep. On being told this, Christina promptly burned the bag of white powder because, she claimed at the time, she was too frightened to use it.

After his initial bout of illness just after Christmas, John Gilmour apparently rallied and felt well enough to travel with his young bride to visit her family farm in Dunlop on New Year's Day 1843. But, following their return on 2 January, the sickness returned – and from then on he grew steadily worse, experiencing tremendous pain in his stomach and bringing up copious amounts of green and yellow slime. After a few days, a doctor was brought in but he was apparently still celebrating the New Year and was somewhat the worse for drink. He diagnosed 'an inflammation', bled Gilmour and ordered him to be rubbed down with turpentine to bring down the fever.

Servants had earlier found a black silk bag in the boiler house near the farmhouse. It contained a small parcel of white powder with the word 'POISON' printed on it and a phial containing some sort of liquid – possibly scent. Servants recognised the bag as belonging to Mrs Gilmour and took it to her. She accepted it from them without a word but it was never seen again. A Renfrewshire druggist testified that on Saturday 7 January he had sold Mrs Gilmour a quantity of arsenic and that she had given him a false name for his records.

A friend of Gilmour visited him on the weekend before he died. He told the court he had known John to be in good health before the marriage but, on this day, his face and eyes were swollen and he was complaining of sharp pains in his chest and side.

Friends spoke of Gilmour's own suspicions about his illness. They told of Gilmour's express wish to be 'opened' (dissected) after his death and they talked about one bout of severe pain when he cried, 'Oh, if ye have given me anything, tell me before I die!'

Although they admitted Mrs Gilmour was extremely attentive to her husband during his illness and that there was no want of kindness, they did recall that she had often stated she was married against her will and that she would have preferred John Anderson as her husband.

The crucial evidence, gleaned by doctors and scientists from the organs taken from Gilmour's corpse, stated that the skin of the cadaver was green in many places over the chest and abdomen and that, although the muscular substance was setting into a glutinous state, the fibres were still intact. It went on, 'The right side was more livid than the left. The chest and abdomen having been laid open, the intestines exhibited a blush all over the external surfaces . . . The lungs were normal. The heart was normal.'

Once their examination was complete, the surgeons were of the opinion that Gilmour had

> died from the effects of an acrid poison, which produced the inflammation of the stomach and bowels . . . and that from the yellow particles on the lining of the stomach, and the yellow patches and streaks in the substances of the stomach and bowels, we suspect that acrid poison to have been arsenic.

The details of the surgical examination, read out coldly and clinically, turned more than a few stomachs but there was worse to come. A succession of grisly exhibits was produced in court and paraded before the judge and jury in glass jars. These included half of the contents of the dead man's stomach, as well as part of his liver, kidney, spleen, oesophagus and the stomach itself. Once this organ recital was over, it was clear to all that John Gilmour had, indeed, been poisoned. But did his wife administer the fatal dose?

At the end of the first day of the trial, the accused's declaration was read to the court. In it, she said that her husband had never told her what he thought had caused his illness but she did claim that he had said that 'I had broken his heart. I suppose he said this because I had told him that he had broken mine: and that I could not feel for him as a wife should do, having been, as was well known, in a manner forced to marry him.'

She admitted buying the arsenic and giving a false name. She admitted dropping the black bag that had been recovered by a servant. She also admitted getting Mary Paterson to buy arsenic on a prior occasion but that she had burned it when she had learned of the effects it would have had. She claimed she had no intention of using the poison on her husband. The arsenic, she said, was to use on herself. She did not love her husband, she was unhappy with her life and she wanted to end it all. However, her mother had found the poison in her pocket and burned it. She also denied feeding Gilmour food and drink laced with the substance and professed to have no idea how it came to be found in his body.

In his summing-up, the Lord Advocate, Duncan McNeill, the Crown Prosecutor, told the jury that Gilmour's death by poisoning was 'as clear as ever had been elicited in any case where a charge of murder was involved'. Someone – either the deceased himself or another person – must have administered the poison. The Lord Advocate felt that sufficient proof existed to implicate the accused. Trapped in a loveless marriage – on her part at least – she had bought the arsenic secretly and admitted possession.

Thomas Maitland, the advocate for the defence, said the case was a matter of life or death for Mrs Gilmour but he disputed whether there was strong legal evidence for a guilty verdict. The evidence was purely circumstantial and, before the jury could be satisfied of her guilt, they had to be convinced that she had harboured feelings of remorseless hatred against her husband. Had she shown such feelings? Had any witnesses testified that she had shown such feelings? He thought not.

He underlined the woman's good character, pointing out she had come from a respectable family. He reminded them that one witness had said she was 'innocent and blameless'. He said she had behaved quite properly and responsibly throughout her husband's illness. Witnesses had further stated she had displayed no excitement or confusion during the crisis. She had never complained of any unkindness on her husband's part in an attempt to justify any action she might have taken. Further, she had placed no restrictions on visitors. Surely, then, the woman deserved the benefit of the doubt?

The fact that John Gilmour kept arsenic in the house was also vital. He used it to kill rats on the farm and, when his new wife took up residence, had his supply removed from the kitchen and placed in a chest in his room. He had already threatened suicide once – when she had refused to marry him. Had Christina's apparent coldness forced him to follow through that threat?

Lord Moncrieff, one of the judges, in his own summing-up, said the jury had been placed in 'one of the most solemn situations in which men could be placed'. He continued:

> It was not only a charge of murder, but it was a charge of murder under circumstances which rendered its perpetration fearful and atrocious. The prisoner was accused of a crime which could only be explained by that depravity of human nature, the mystery of which Man cannot penetrate.
>
> A fearful, more unnatural deed was never laid to the charge of a human being.

He then went on to advise the jury on the legalities of the case, going over some points of evidence. His remarks were generally impartial but some statements did seem to lean slightly towards Christina Gilmour's innocence. The jury was out for an hour.

Journalists were prevented by a court order from reporting on the trial until the following week, when the *Glasgow Courier* stated:

> On Friday she sat for hours with a cup of water in her hands. Under the circumstances there was a remarkable degree of coldness or listlessness about her; and she heard the verdict of the jury – which to her was life or death – without the slightest sensible emotion.

There was a breathless hush as the Clerk read out the verdict. 'The jury, after a careful and mature consideration of the evidence brought before them in this case, are unanimously of the opinion that John Gilmour died from the effects of arsenic.' Then there was a pause, deepening the tension already felt in the courtroom. Eyes turned to the dock where the black-clad Mrs Gilmour sat stock-still. The Clerk continued, 'But find it not proved against the prisoner at the bar, as libelled.'

Spectators in the public gallery erupted in approval at the verdict. The cheering reached such a pitch that the judge was forced to quieten them by wielding threats of contempt.

Christina Gilmour left the courtroom with the same blank expression she had shown throughout the trial. She displayed no sign of relief, no sign of victory. The mask she had donned the day she was arrested never once slipped. She left Edinburgh that night on the 10 p.m. train, arriving in Glasgow at midnight. From there, she returned to Ayrshire.

She did not marry John Anderson but wore the widow's weeds until she died at the age of eighty-seven in Stewarton, Ayrshire. The not proven verdict is often seen as relaying the message that 'We know you did it but can't quite prove it so go away and don't do it again.' Perhaps John Anderson feared that, if he ever stepped out of line or if Christina discovered that she did not love him quite as much as she thought, he too might suddenly take ill.

Thirteen years later, in Glasgow, another attractive young Scots-woman created excitement when she faced charges of murder by arsenic. She was Madeleine Smith and the prosecution claimed that she had laced the hot chocolate of her former lover, Pierre L'Angelier, with the powder after he became something of an embarrassment to her. Her case was also found not proven.

Perhaps Christina Gilmour read of this in her Ayrshire home and smiled.

MOTHERS' RUIN

Scots law took a dim view of immorality. Killing or robbing someone was bad enough and the law, as we have seen, lost no time in exacting payment. However, there was nothing like sex for getting the populace hot and sweaty – and not necessarily in a good way. Morality was dictated by the Church, be it Roman or Reformed, and the twin evils of adultery and fornication were stamped on heavily. Church laws were made by Man and enforced by men. In Scotland, their rigid disciplines were a whip wielded by an iron hand to scourge the backs of the unworthy, the unchristian and the immoral.

Prior to the Reformation, Roman Catholic bishops were entitled to seize the goods and lands of any man caught doing the wild thing with a woman who was not his wife. Of course, if that person made a generous donation to the Church, then they could happily forget all about those sins.

After the Reformation, other punishments were introduced. Fines were levied, for they were a lucrative way of raising funds for Kirk or Crown. As we have already seen, guilty parties could be forced to don sackcloth, sit on the 'cutty stool' in front of the congregation or hang from the 'jougs' (neck manacles bolted to the exterior of churches) for all to see. If they refused to plead for forgiveness for their sins, they could be excommunicated, which meant they could not work, marry, baptise their children or, ultimately, have a decent burial and their misdemeanours could also be referred to the courts for criminal charges. They could be banished from the town or city for a set period of time, put in the stocks with their heads shaved or have their flesh pierced and burned, their backs flayed and scourged and their bodies abused and beaten. They could also be hanged.

And, if a woman was unlucky enough to fall pregnant 'without benefit of clergy', the repercussions could be dire. For, in the eyes of the Kirk, the unmarried mother – and she alone – was responsible and the resultant damage to her reputation was catastrophic. Women could be publicly rebuked and reviled either on the cutty stool or at the pillar – a raised area at the front of the church. And the disgrace and associated danger to their livelihoods was such that many tried to hide the signs of any pregnancy and even the birth itself. In those days, having a baby was a risky enough business even with the aid of experienced midwives and doctors. Without such assistance, the chances of a miscarriage or stillbirth increased significantly. The temptation to avoid disgrace, not only by hiding any signs of pregnancy but also by murdering the child, was evident.

In 1690, an act was passed against Concealment of Pregnancy. Basically, it stated that, if a woman hid her condition and if the child was later found to be dead or missing, the punishment was death by hanging or at the stake.

Prior to that, in 1614, Janet Brown appeared in Edinburgh after hiding her newly-born child in a dry-stone wall near Biggar in Lanarkshire. The charge was that she had strangled the baby but she claimed that it had been stillborn. It did not matter much anyway, for she was still guilty of concealing her pregnancy. She was hanged on Castle Hill and all her goods were forfeited to the Crown.

In 1690, Kirk ministers reportedly enjoyed the sight of three women being hanged for child murder. One, Margaret Inglis, appeared unrepentant. The second, Bessie Turnbull, had already shown remorse and had actually brought her crime to light by confessing. The third, Christian Adams, had kept the fact she was 'with child' a secret for fear that it would ruin her lover, as he was a married man. To protect him – and herself – she had smothered the child and buried it in a field.

In Aberdeen in 1752, former servant Christian Phren threw her newborn child on to a fire. She was caught and driven in a cart to the gallows – then sited on a hill near to what is now Pittodrie Stadium – with the scorched remains of her victim in an apron. Her body hung in chains until anatomy students took it away for dissection.

In 1763, Jean Cameron, servant to a Dundee excise officer, found herself pregnant to soldier Alexander MacGregor. Out of fear of losing her job, she hid her condition and then murdered the baby. She was hanged in Perth on 19 October.

In the same year, Margaret Douglas, servant to a Captain John McKenzie in Ross-shire, was called before the Kirk session for being 'debauched' by another servant, Alexander McKenzie – the second time she had been caught for such an offence. This time she actually gave birth while walking along a road and later said that she had not known whether the bairn was alive or dead when she had wrapped it in linen and hidden it under a stone. However, on returning to her employer's home, it was deemed obvious that she had indeed given birth, a fact confirmed by a midwife. Margaret was arrested, tried, found guilty and sentenced to death. On the gallows at Inverness, she confessed to a previous murder – that of the son of a previous employer. No one at the time had suspected foul play and she said that she had done it just because she had taken a dislike to the lad.

But not all murdering mothers were executed. In 1736, sisters Helen and Isobel Walker were living with their widowed mother in Kirkpatrick Irongray, Dumfriesshire. Isobel fell pregnant but hid the fact from her family and drowned the newborn babe in Cluden Water. However, as luck would have it, heavy rains gorged the river and the little body was washed ashore. A handkerchief round the tiny corpse's neck was identified as Isobel's. The authorities forced her to undergo the Ordeal by Touch, in which an accused person was forced to touch their alleged victim to see what happened. Isobel did not disappoint them. As the dead child was laid on her knees, she threw a fit and was arrested immediately.

Her sister, a devout Christian, was asked to swear on the bible as to whether she had known Isobel was pregnant. With her hand on the Holy Scripture, she could not lie – not even for her sister whom she loved – so she answered truthfully in the negative. However, while Isobel lay in the Edinburgh Tolbooth awaiting execution, Helen walked to London to appeal for a pardon. She managed to find the ear of the Duke of Argyll, who was so moved by her impassioned speech that he spoke to the king and arranged a royal pardon, on the guarantee that Isobel would leave Scotland and never return. The gallant Helen Walker was the inspiration behind Sir Walter Scott's character, Jeannie Deans, in his novel *The Heart of Midlothian*. He later arranged for a stone to be erected over her grave in Kirkpatrick Irongray churchyard.

In 1803, the penalty for concealing a pregnancy was reduced to transportation but the shame of illegitimacy lived on throughout the century and well into the next. In 2002, evidence came to light of a tragic situation on the Orkney Islands when workmen renovating a house in Harray recovered the bones of three infants. The children were believed to have been drowned by their grandmother. The practice, it seems, was fairly common on the islands. In fact, when the case reached the national press, it was claimed that workmen over the years often used to find bones buried in cellars and simply reburied them. In this particular case, it was believed that these children, all illegitimate and born in the early part of the twentieth century, were not allowed to draw much of a breath before being consigned to buckets of water by grandmother Tomima Gray. Their mother, Violet Gray, was said to have been a prostitute who returned to her mother's cottage whenever she fell pregnant. Here the family shame was always treated in the same way – although it is possible that the children had been stillborn.

But Violet's fourth childbirth proved complicated and, because a doctor had to be called, the baby, a boy called Gordon, was saved. He had to spend the first few years of his life locked away in the attic, for fear that Grannie Tomima might wish him harm, and he did not learn his early history until Violet told him about it on her deathbed in the 1950s. Gordon died in 1995. Although forensic evidence failed to link the bones of the three less fortunate infants conclusively to the Gray family, the Grays were allowed to have them buried.

But not everyone took such drastic steps to cover up a pregnancy. Putting illegitimate children up for adoption became a common occurrence in Scotland and beyond and, naturally, it was not long before the more enterprising individuals realised that there was a profit to be made from this. They called the trade 'baby farming' and, in the late 1880s, a woman in Edinburgh made the business public when she was accused of not one child murder but three.

9

KING'S EVIDENCE

Jessie King, 1887-9

In the autumn and winter of 1888, the archetypal serial killer was stalking the dingy back streets of London's East End, leaving a succession of dead prostitutes and an everlasting mystery in his wake. Jack the Ripper's motives and identity remain unknown but his nickname lives on through the years and it has spawned a mini-industry of books, TV programmes and films.

In Scotland during the same period, another serial killer was operating but there is little mystery over her motives and none at all over her identity. She operated in Edinburgh but, unlike Burke and Hare, she did not haunt the mean streets of the Old Town looking for her victims. They were handed to her willingly and she was even paid to take them. Those victims were the unwanted children of working mothers. They were often born and taken away in secret because their mothers feared losing their jobs, having their lives interrupted and being stigmatised by society. They called her a 'baby farmer' but she was nothing less than a child-killer.

The woman went to her death worrying over her own soul and its salvation, prayers dripping from her lips like tears of self-pity. But what of her little victims? Three deaths were lodged at her door but it is widely believed that others had gone unnoticed and unmourned. They had come into the world with nothing and left the world with even less – no mother, no father, no one to grieve for them, no one to remember them. Who, then, prayed for the lost ones? For the babies who had been conceived in passion and disposed of in haste, to be hidden from a society that would not accept them? Who prayed for them?

Walter Anderson Campbell was born on 20 March 1887 in Preston-pans, East Lothian. He was illegitimate and his mother, Elizabeth Campbell, claimed that the father was a Leith postman named David Ferguson Finlay. However, within days of the baby's birth, Elizabeth herself was dead and the boy was left in the care of her sister, Janet Anderson, who approached the father and offered to adopt the child if she was given money. Finlay refused although he did provide financial support for three months while he advertised the boy in newspapers for adoption. This was a common practice and, at the time, completely legal.

A Mrs Stewart replied and Finlay called at her rooms at 24 Dalkeith Road, Edinburgh, to meet both her and her father. The woman explained that her own child had died soon after childbirth and she was desperate for another so Finlay agreed to let them have his son and gave them £5. Mrs Stewart and her father then travelled to Prestonpans to collect the child from Janet Anderson.

No one knows what happened to Walter after that. Neighbours in Dalkeith Road believed that the couple, whom Finlay had thought were father and daughter, were actually uncle and niece. And their name was not Stewart but Pearson. Over a year later, one local tenant confirmed that a little boy had arrived in the flat in August 1887 but that three months later he was gone. The boy had been noticeably ill, said the neighbour, but the woman she knew as Pearson said he was her sister's child and had been sent home. Soon after that the Pearsons moved from Dalkeith Road.

No trace of little Walter was ever found. He had, without doubt, fallen victim to the scandal of baby farming in which women, often midwives, took unwanted children off the parents' hands in return for a fee. Usually the woman would 'farm out' the child for adoption, either selling the baby on or paying someone else to take it. Sometimes the child found its way to a kind and loving family. Baby Walter, though, was not so fortunate. At some point during his stay in Dalkeith Road, he was killed and his murderer escaped detection for a further year.

But her name was not Stewart or Pearson. It was Jessie King. And the killing would not stop with that little boy.

Jessie King was born in the Anderston area of Glasgow in 1861. For a time, she worked in the city's mills but did not find the work to her taste. So she left the city of her birth and travelled east to the nation's capital, where she found employment in Causewayside as a laundry worker. However, by 1887 she was homeless and pregnant. Around this time, fifty-nine-year-old labourer Thomas Pearson agreed to take her in, 'Out of pity,' he said. He may not have been the father of the child but he agreed to put a roof over her head as long as she took care of the place and made him comfortable. 'Making him comfortable' would almost certainly come to mean providing him with sexual favours.

The child died soon after birth but King was desperate to be a mother. It was soon after this that they saw David Finlay's advertisement and they replied. King got what she wanted – and made some cash in the process – but her maternal instincts did not last long for, according to Pearson, he came home from work one day to find the lad gone. King told him she was tired of him and had put him in a home. She also said she wanted to return to work and the presence of the child was proving inconvenient.

But these were lies. She had killed the boy. How she did it is unknown. What she did with the body is unknown. Exactly how many children went through King's hands is unknown. In the end, she faced charges regarding only three – and then it was only because she had been sloppy in disposing of one poor waif's body.

A young boy, named Alexander Brown, unwittingly set in motion the forces that uncovered the scandal. In early October 1888, the eleven-year-old was playing with friends in Cheyne Street in the Stockbridge area of Edinburgh when he came across a parcel wrapped in a piece of oilskin coat lying beside the door of a back green. One of his friends gave the bundle a severe kick and, when it burst open, young Alexander saw the remains of a dead baby boy.

The boys ran to a nearby street and found Constable George Stewart. He accompanied them back to Cheyne Street where he gingerly lifted the grisly little bundle. Such news, even in a city hardened by many outrages over the decades, was difficult to contain. As the police officer carried the corpse through the streets, a host of women clustered around him, many weeping over the fate of the poor wee bairn. But one woman stood out. Constable Stewart spotted her at the door of number 10 Cheyne Street. Of all the women, she was the only one who appeared uninterested and unmoved by the tragedy.

The news reached the ears of local landlord James Banks and his wife Jane. They recalled a tenant, a Mrs Pearson, who had one day turned up with a baby – that time it had been female – claiming that she had been given £25 to take the little girl off the hands of an unmarried mother. Lately, though, the child was nowhere to be seen and, when asked about this, Mrs Pearson told the landlord that she had managed to find someone who would take the child for £18.

Mr and Mrs Banks felt the tenant's conduct to be sufficiently suspicious that they passed it on to the police. Subsequently, Detective Officers James Clark and David Simpson were sent to interview the so-called Mrs Pearson, living at 10 Cheyne Street. Because the dead child was male and the baby seen by Mr Banks had been female, the two police officers perhaps looked on this as a mere formality. However, if there is one rule in detection it is that nothing should be overlooked. Their visit would eventually ensnare a baby-killer.

They asked the woman about the child she had shown Mr Banks and she admitted immediately that she'd had such an infant in her care. The baby's name was Violet Tomlinson, she said, and she still had her authentic birth certificate in her possession. The documentation showed the child had been born in August.

The detectives asked her, 'Where did you get the child from?'

'From her mother,' was her reply. 'Her name is Alice Tomlinson and she got herself in the family way and gave birth in Edinburgh's maternity hospital. After a week, she let it be known that she wanted someone to adopt the child.'

'And you volunteered?'

'Yes,' she replied. 'She gave me £2 to take the child and a further £25 for her keep.'

'Where is the baby now?' the detectives continued.

'With my sister,' she answered. 'Her husband's the piper to the Duke of Montrose, you know. Alice Tomlinson's mother knows all about it.'

Officer Clark diligently visited the elder Tomlinson woman and asked her about the transaction. Although everything Mrs Pearson had said was confirmed, he remained uneasy. There was something not quite right about her story, something just slightly off. She looked respectable enough, she sounded convincing, but he could not shake off the feeling in his gut that she was hiding something. So he went back to the house in Cheyne Street and asked if he could search the place, particularly a cupboard that, for some reason, had caught his interest. Mrs Pearson tried to stop him but the policeman was not to be dissuaded – in fact, her resistance only made him all the more suspicious. Finally, the woman agreed, her body slumping as she muttered, 'Get a cab and take me to the police office. It's there. I did it!'

These words and what he found in the cupboard proved the policeman was right to be insistent. There were two shelves in the cupboard and, on the bottom one, he found the body of a baby girl, perhaps around six weeks old, wrapped in canvass. He also found a fragment of oilskin, similar to the one that had acted as the first dead baby's shroud, and a canister of chloride of lime, used to mask the stench of putrefaction. It was also commonly held that lime would speed up the decomposition process but, in actual fact, it acted more as a preservative.

Professor of Medical Jurisprudence and Chief Police Surgeon Dr Henry Littlejohn, one of the pioneers of forensic medicine, performed the post-mortem on the little boy found in Cheyne Street. His son, Harvey – who would also become something of a legend in his chosen profession – assisted him. The body weighed in at 11 lb 4 oz and was 29 ins in length. After removing the oilskin, they found that the body had been wrapped in cotton so tightly that it had caused the flesh to mummify and had halted any real decomposition although, when unwrapped, the skin was covered in patches of white mould. The cotton was carefully peeled away from the head to reveal strong discolouration of the face. The cause of that was all too obvious – an apron string tied so tightly around the neck that it bit deeply into the skin.

At first, it was difficult to ascertain the gender of the child because the sexual organs had melded together during the mummification process but, after several hours of soaking in warm water, they were able to determine that the child was male and around one year of age. They estimated he had been killed six months before.

Dr Littlejohn also examined the female child found by Officer Clark. She was 23 ins in length and weighed in at 8 lb 1 oz. Although she had not been dead for as long as the first child, decomposition was at an advanced stage – when the body was opened he found a considerable number of maggots and flies feasting on the flesh. Like the first body, there was a ligature, this time a piece of cloth, wrapped around the neck twice and pulled so tightly that it had cut a deep furrow in the flesh. However, Dr Littlejohn believed the cause of death to be suffocation, perhaps by a hand placed over the mouth or after the child had choked on a quantity of whisky it had been given.

He was assisted in this second autopsy by a man who became the inspiration for the greatest of all fictional detectives – Sherlock Holmes. Dr Joseph Bell was Professor of Medicine at Edinburgh University and taught the young medical student Arthur Conan Doyle, Sherlock Holmes' celebrated creator. There was, however, little need for Dr Bell's acute deductive mind in this case, for Mrs Pearson – or, rather, Jessie King – was making a full confession.

She did so, she said later, because she believed that, by revealing all, she would escape the gallows.

The dead boy's name was Alexander Gunn and Jessie King had taken him for adoption from his mother Catherine Whyte of Edinburgh's Canonmills area, receiving £3 for taking the baby off her hands. Alexander was one of twins born to the domestic servant on 1 May 1887 in the home of a Mrs Mitchell. The mother had given the boys to a nurse, a Mrs McKay, to look after but soon realised she could not afford to support them so had agreed to put them up for adoption. The twin boys had been split up, with one, named Robert, going to a Mrs Henderson while Alexander had gone to Jessie King, this time using the name MacPherson. Catherine Whyte had tried many times to see her child and had failed but Mrs McKay had told her he was doing well.

Soon afterwards, Catherine Whyte married but she did not tell her new husband about having given birth to twins. When the scandal blew up, she proved unwilling to discuss the matter with the authorities for fear that her husband and new friends would hear. According to a medical report, the matter 'acted on her nervous system' and brought on a breakdown that led to her being admitted to hospital.

Thomas Pearson was, at first, unhappy with the arrangement as he felt that they were hard pressed enough to take care of themselves. However, when he heard that Jessie had been given some money to keep the boy, he relented and said the child could stay for a few weeks. As time went on, he became quite fond of the lad, whom they called Cluny. They told anyone who asked that the child belonged to her sister who was ill.

By May 1888, King found she could not cope with the child and tried to have him taken by a children's home. However, the management, with all the sanctimony that Victorian family values could muster, refused to consider illegitimate youngsters and King was sent away. Finally, in a drunken rage, she strangled the boy with her apron string. She could not support the child, she said, and it was the best thing in the long run. When Pearson asked where the boy was, however, she told him that she'd managed to place him in a home. But when Pearson said, once or twice, that they should go and visit the boy, she fobbed him off with excuses.

The body was wrapped in part of an oilskin coat belonging to Pearson – to keep in the smell, she later said – and placed in a locked box. When Pearson asked what had happened to the coat, she told him that she had thrown it out because it was covered in green mould. The next day she took the body out of the box and stored it in a cupboard. At that time she and Pearson were living in Ann's Court, Canonmills, and three days after killing the boy, she removed the corpse again and carried it to Stockbridge where she hid it in the basement of a house. It lay there for four months until the beginning of October, when she retrieved it for the last time and dumped it in Cheyne Street.

Telling people she had given the child out for nursing, Jessie King carried on as if nothing had happened. A local girl who had actually looked after little Alexander for a period was told that the boy had been taken away by his father. The girl, thirteen-year-old Janet Binnie, recalled being told by King that the child actually belonged to 'her man's sister', who had died of cancer of the womb. King had told young Janet that she had never liked the dead woman and was none too fond of her child either and Janet admitted that she often saw King slapping the infant.

Whether out of love or as a matter of fact, King exonerated Thomas Pearson from any involvement in the murders. According to her, Pearson had not even known that the Tomlinson baby was in the house. The mother had paid King £2 to care for her and, on the afternoon she brought the baby home, she had given the child whisky to quieten her. However, the brew proved too strong and the baby choked. She did not want Pearson to know the little one was there, so she placed her hand over her mouth to stifle the crying. In so doing, she silenced little Violet forever. She put the body in the cupboard and, as she had to go out, stuffed a cloth into her mouth in case she revived.

Pearson, though, was identified as the Mr Stewart who had

posed as Jessie's father when little Walter Campbell was brought for adoption. From the moment of his arrest at Lawson's Nursery in Ferry Road, where he was employed as a gardener, Pearson insisted he was an innocent man. He told police – and later the High Court – that Jessie said Walter Campbell had been put in a home because she was tired of him. She also told him Alexander Gunn had been placed with Miss Stirling's Home – which often sent orphans abroad – because she could not cope with him. Pearson had wanted to visit him at the home but Jessie told him they could only call at certain times. And he claimed he had not been aware little Violet had ever been in the house.

He did admit using the name MacPherson on occasion and passing himself off as Jessie's uncle. He confirmed that Jessie sometimes used the name Stewart and that he went along with it because he was her friend.

Although no real defence was raised during her trial in February 1889, King's counsel attempted to paint Pearson as the real mastermind behind the baby-farming scandal. It was alleged that he was the one who influenced her into committing these dreadful acts. However, her own declaration, given in the presence of a lawyer, had absolved Pearson from any knowledge of the murders and had confirmed that she had acted on her own. At any rate, Pearson was given immunity from prosecution as long as he told the truth on the stand.

The judge described the case as being 'as sad and as piteous a picture of society life as ever came before a Court of Justice'. Unsurprisingly, the jury did not take long to reach their verdict. The fifteen men were out for a total of just three minutes. She had originally been charged with three counts of murder – Alexander Gunn, Violet Tomlinson and Walter Campbell. However, with no body and very little evidence of foul play, the third charge was dropped. But she was found unanimously guilty of the first two killings.

Jessie King appeared calm as she stood to hear the sentence but the muscles at the side of her mouth were jerking and twitching furiously. The Lord Justice Clerk stared down at her from the bench and said:

> Jessie King, no one who has listened to the evidence at this trial can fail to be satisfied that the jury could have come to any other conclusion than that arrived at in your case.
>
> Your days are now numbered.
>
> Remember, the sentence of this court and the penalty of law after that sentence relate to this world and this world only. I entreat you to be persuaded not to harden your heart against the influence of the world to come. All that you have done can be blotted out for the world to come if you will but repent and turn from your sins. I beseech you to attend to the ministrations you will receive; and as you confessed your crimes in your declaration to Man, so you will confess to God also. You will be sure of forgiveness.

Having thus addressed her spiritual needs, the judge turned to her corporeal future. 'Now it is my sad duty to pronounce the penalty of the law; and I and all who hear me, will join in the prayer that you will be led to true repentance and so to salvation.' He then placed the black cap on his head and informed her she would be hanged on Monday 11 March 1889 in Calton Jail.

During his speech, Jessie King's composure cracked and her groans echoed round the courtroom. Her hysteria grew while his lecture about her future deliverance was being made and, when he finally announced the death sentence, she screamed and fainted in the dock. Two police officers carried her bodily to the cells below the courtroom from where she was transported to the condemned cell of Calton Jail.

She was to be the first woman to hang in Scotland since 1862, when Mary Reid, or Timney, had been convicted for beating her neighbour to death (*see* p. 144). However, there were many in the city who believed she should be spared. Attempts were made to have the sentence commuted to life, with 2,000 residents of Stockbridge even submitting a petition stating she was 'a weak-minded person and ought not be to held entirely responsible for her actions'. The petition was sent to the Secretary of State for Scotland, the Marquis of Lothian, along with medical reports regarding the state of her mind. But the Marquis was not in a forgiving mood. As there was no doubt over her guilt, he said, the law must take its course. He went on to say that as the offence 'was a very heinous one, there would probably be little sorrow among the community at large over her future'.

There were newspaper reports that King tried to cheat the hangman although this was later denied by her priest. A long pin was found in her cell at one time, which she claimed was for picking her teeth, but officials believed she had a more lethal function in mind. Later, a length of rope was found. No one knew how she came into possession of these items but there was little doubt that she planned to do herself some mischief. At some stage, she had also either given birth to another child, which would perhaps have been Pearson's, or she had taken charge of another adoptee. A letter from the governor to the procurator fiscal and dated 18 January 1889 reads:

> I beg to inform you that Jessie King, an untried prisoner confined here on a warrant at your instance, attempted to commit suicide last night by strangulation.
>
> I am of the opinion that she means to take her own life *and that of her child* [my italics] but every precaution will be taken to prevent this. In the meantime the child has, on the recommendation of the surgeon, been removed from her.

It seems that, on this occasion, she had taken a length of tape from the child's pinafore and wrapped it round her own neck several times. In a note to the governor, the prison doctor, Henry Hay, said he had ensured King was

> most carefully attended night and day as she seemed to be labouring under mental excitement and evidently means to commit suicide.

From what she has said to the other two prisoners associated with her, I consider it unsafe to allow her child to be in the cell with her.

Edinburgh's Lord Provost was technically responsible for organising the execution but he delegated the job to Baillies McDonald and Steel. McDonald, though, wanted nothing to do with the killing of a woman, whether she deserved it or not, and respectfully asked to be relieved of the onerous duty. It then fell to a Baillie Russell who had no such qualms.

The actual scaffold was built in a corridor running between the male and female sections of the jail. The days of executions being public spectacles were long gone and the scene of Jessie King's final minutes would be hidden from non-official eyes.

The executioner was Yorkshireman James Berry, a former policeman and shoe salesman from Bradford, whose deeply held religious convictions did not prevent him from dropping a number of murderers in England and Scotland. His first such commission had actually come from the City of Edinburgh five years earlier when he had executed two miners turned poachers, William Innes and Robert Vickers, who had been convicted of murdering two gamekeepers. The success of that double hanging had brought him work in England, his first execution south of the Border having been that of a woman in Lincoln. Mary Lefley had poisoned her husband with arsenic disguised in a rice pudding. But the convicted woman had not gone quietly into the long night and her screams had distressed Berry so much that, forever after, he was loath to hang a female. His record was also marred by a few botched executions – including one where the accused's head was snapped from its neck by the drop – and the pressure of his job brought on a nervous breakdown in 1888.

However, he arrived in Edinburgh on Friday 8 March 1889 to take up temporary lodgings in the jail while he made his calculations. He ascertained her weight as 7 st. 2 lb and calculated that the job would require a 6 ft 6 in. drop if his favoured Italian hemp rope was to be used.

137

Jessie King had clearly been listening to the judge's advice for, throughout her last night, she 'paid great attention to the ministrations of her spiritual advisers' – in her case Canon Donlevy and two Franciscan nuns. She went to bed at 11 p.m. but did not fall asleep until around 12.30 a.m. and she was awake again by 5 a.m. on the Monday morning, the day of her execution. An hour later, Canon Donlevy was leading a mass in the prison chapel and administering the sacrament to the penitent woman.

After a breakfast of bread and butter, boiled eggs and tea, she was left to prepare herself for what was to come. Meanwhile, the proprieties of legal murder were being observed in another part of the prison. At around 7 a.m., a large knot of men – including doctors, police officers, the prison chaplain and various prison and court officials, as well as journalists – strode through the corridors to the office of the prison matron. At a few minutes before 8 a.m., the prison governor made the following request:

> Baillies Russell and Steel, magistrates of the City of Edinburgh, would you have the goodness to proceed to the prisoner's cell and identify her with the warrant in order that she may be handed over to you for execution as required by law?

Then, because a job isn't over until the paperwork is done, he added, 'And, perhaps, on your return, you will be good enough to sign the receipt.'

The receipt in question read:

> HM Prison, Edinburgh, 11th March 1889 – Received by the governor of HM Prison, Edinburgh, the person of convict Jessie King, with a view to the carrying out of the sentence of death which was passed in High Court of Justiciary, held in Edinburgh on the 18th February 1889, as per the extract conviction exhibited here.

Jessie King walked with Canon Donlevy and prison officials from the condemned cell into the execution area. By now, she had calmly accepted her fate. She thanked the prison staff for the kindness they had shown her and bade goodbye to a number of female officers. As she walked, the priest murmured the litany and she made the correct responses. There was no gallows platform as such so there were no steps for her to climb to the noose. Berry preferred to slip the hood over the head of his subjects before they reached the trapdoor, as he believed the sight of the dangling rope was unsettling. Jessie stood quietly as he covered her face and pinioned her arms and legs. Then she was led to the trapdoor where the looped rope hung from a nine-foot gibbet and beam. The accused woman said, 'Into thy hands, oh Lord, I commend my spirit. Lord Jesus, receive my soul. Jesus, son of David, have mercy on me.'

At three minutes past eight, Berry released the trapdoor and Jessie King's body jerked into the darkness below. The satisfied hangman said that she never moved after the drop. He also opined that she was the bravest woman he 'had ever had under [him]'.

When the reporters were admitted to the chamber, they found Berry staring into the gaping trap. Given his distaste for hanging women, he appeared more relaxed than he was probably feeling. A pale Canon Donlevy stood nearby, tightly clutching his crucifix. King's body swung gently, the creaking of the rope unnaturally loud. The law demanded that the body hang there for a period of one hour before it could be taken down and buried in an unmarked grave within the prison walls.

Outside those walls, between 1,500 and 2,000 people waited for news of the execution. They had been gathering since the sun began to glimmer. Their breath was visible in the frosty March air and the women and girls clutched their shawls to their heads to try to keep out the cold. They stood on the North Bridge, on Regent Road and around Nelson's Column on Calton Hill, their eyes trained on the prison towers. They were from every stratum of society, the clean and the tidy rubbing shoulders with the unkempt and the unwashed who had streamed from Canongate and Cowgate to their chosen vantage points. Barrow boys and street vendors suspended trade to stand on their boxes and carts to gain a better view of the flagpole from which the black flag of death would be flown. They waited patiently, with no sign of the carnival atmosphere that would have attended so many hangings in the past, as the chilly air echoed only occasionally to the tolling of the prison bell. A church clock chimed the eighth hour and, a few short minutes later, a murmur grew among them as the black flag fluttered up the mast. The crowd looked at the signal for a few moments then began to disperse as silently as it had gathered – the gentleman with the washer woman, the shopkeeper with the street sweeper, the rich man, the poor man, the beggar man and the thief, all heading back to the town houses and the wynds and the closes that made up the city.

They left knowing that Jessie King, the baby-killer, had 'passed to her account'. They did not know that she would be the last woman to be hanged in Edinburgh.

PLATFORM PARTIES

Scottish courts were never as keen on sentencing women to death as their English counterparts. But, as we have already seen, of course, that did not mean they would not do so.

In the Middle Ages, Scots barons were granted the power of pit and gallows by the king and, because proper records were either never kept or no longer exist, it is difficult to say how many women were drowned, strangled, burned or hanged at the fancy of the laird or his often corrupt bailiffs.

Hanging was not the science it later became. Each district had its dule, or hanging, tree and offenders were made to stand on a cart – the rope thrown over a branch, the noose around the neck – before the cart was driven away, leaving them to die a slow, agonising death. Sometimes men would simply haul them up on a rope looped around their necks, holding them there until they died.

Executions became public carnivals, with street vendors hawking their wares and, as in the case of William Burke, decent vantage points being rented out to the upper classes who had no great desire to rub shoulders with the great unwashed.

It was not only serious crimes like murder for which men and women could be executed. In Inveraray in 1752, Anne Campbell was hanged for the theft of £50 while, at her side, was eighty-year-old Sarah Graham who had made off with £900 in IOUs. Jean Craig was another thief and she met her doom in Aberdeen, in 1784, while housebreaker Elspeth Reid should have dangled on the same day but received a respite due to her pregnancy. However, six months later she kept her date with the hangman. Jean Scott was a Glasgow thief and housebreaker executed in 1784. Elizabeth Paul was another Glaswegian who had been banished from the city for theft and then flogged through the streets when she showed her face again. She should have 'taken a telling' for, in 1786 she was hanged for stealing four pieces of cloth. In 1817, Irishwoman Margaret Crossan was found guilty of wilful fire-raising during which twelve cows, a bull and three calves died. She was hanged in Ayr, along with two men found guilty of robbery and theft, in the town's only triple execution.

Although Scottish courts were never as keen on executing women as their English counterparts, they still managed to make mistakes. One woman who may have been innocent but who met her doom on the scaffold was Margaret Tyndall, or Shuttleworth, in 1821. She had been found guilty of murdering her vintner husband by beating him to death with a poker. No motive was provided for the crime and the evidence was sparse – apart from the fact that the accused was alone in the house with the deceased at the time of the murder and all the doors and windows were locked. She had, however, been dead drunk that night and had been put to bed by a servant, who later went out to attend, fittingly, a wake.

Despite denying her guilt continually, Margaret Shuttleworth was hanged on 7 December and her body given over for dissection. However, some years later, a tramp, charged with another murder, confessed to killing Mr Shuttleworth. He had placed the bloody poker beside the woman as she lay in a drunken stupor and then escaped from the house by climbing up the wide chimney.

Obviously, not every woman executed in Scotland was innocent or even guilty of a comparatively trivial crime. Agnes Dougal was described as an 'atrocious woman who lived a very lewd and violent life'. She was the mother of four children – all illegitimate – whose downfall came when a suitor said that he would only marry her if her eight-year-old daughter, Joanna Finlay, was out of the picture. During a walk along the River Clyde, just as they passed the then village of Anderston, Dougal attacked the girl and cut her throat so deeply that she almost severed the head from the body. She was hanged in November 1767.

Seven years later, Margaret Adams and her sister, Agnes, broke into the shop of their neighbour, Janet Mcintyre, in Glasgow's Argyle Street and murdered her. They were heard, though, and found hiding under the bed. Margaret was hanged in Edinburgh in 1774 but Agnes was reprieved.

In Paisley in 1793, Agnes White murdered her five-year-old child by feeding it milk laced with oil of vitriol. She was hanged in Glasgow.

In 1823, Mary McKinnon, who managed an Edinburgh brothel, was hanged for stabbing a solicitor's clerk. It was estimated that 20,000 people turned out to witness her death on the Lawnmarket.

In Arbroath, jealous Margaret Wishart poisoned her blind sister in order to win the affections of their handsome lodger. She was hanged in Forfar in 1827, pleading her innocence.

After an argument, Euphemia Lawson and her husband, Hugh McMillan, attacked a neighbour and threw sulphuric acid over him. Although he subsequently died, they were brought to court on charges of attempted murder. The man was acquitted but the woman was sentenced to death. She was hanged in Edinburgh on 23 January 1828.

In October 1830, Catherine Humphrey became the first woman to hang in Aberdeen in forty-five years. She and her husband had not been getting along. She had often threatened to do him harm and her husband predicted she would die 'facing Marischal Street', a reference to the site of the gallows at the time. She was convicted for poisoning him with oil of vitriol.

In 1838, Carluke woman Mrs Jaffray saw to it that the wearing of Rob Roy tartan went out of fashion by wearing a shawl bearing the red and black plaid to the gallows. She had been found guilty of poisoning two lodgers with arsenic.

In 1850, Mary Lennox died on the rope in Glasgow after poisoning her sister-in-law at Strathaven. She fainted on the scaffold and had to be held up from either side as the hangman drew the bolt that opened the trapdoor.

Probably one of the most interesting platform parties took place in Glasgow in August 1853. Hans McFarlane and Helen Blackwood had been found guilty of murdering ship's carpenter Alexander Boyd by throwing him from the window of a building. With echoes of John and Catherine Stuart and their liking for 'Dr' laudanum (*see* p. 97), they first made him insensible with whisky, mixed this time with snuff, then robbed him. While in Duke Street Prison, McFarlane asked for permission to marry his lover, Blackwood. Permission was refused but they were determined to be man and wife. As they stood on the scaffold near to Glasgow's South Prison on the site of the present-day High Court, McFarlane announced to the woman – and the 40,000-strong crowd there to see them hang – 'Helen Blackwood, before God and in the presence of these witnesses I take you to be my wife. Do you consent?'

The woman replied, 'I do.'

McFarlane then said, 'Then before these witnesses I declare you to be what you have always been to me, a true and faithful wife, and you die an honest woman.'

The minister officiating at the hanging then said, 'Amen', the bolt was drawn and the newly married pair fell to their deaths.

Condemned people often hoped for a last-minute reprieve, searching the crowds for a man bearing a letter from the authorities that would commute their sentence to life imprisonment or transportation. Such was the case of Mary Reid, or Timney, who, in 1862, was found guilty of murdering her neighbour, Ann Hannah, by battering her to death in Carsphairn in what is now Dumfries and Galloway. The mother of four insisted she had struck out in self- defence but efforts to have the death sentence reduced failed. However, just as the trap was to be sprung, a man appeared with a letter for the prison governor. The woman's spirits rose as he opened it, believing that this was the long-hoped-for reprieve, but they were cruelly shattered again when it was revealed to be merely a request from a London news agency for a speedy report of the execution. With a cry of, 'Oh, my four weans,' Mary Timney was judicially murdered.

Jessie McLachlan was luckier for her sentence was commuted to life in prison. She had been convicted of murdering domestic servant Jessie McPherson in Glasgow, in 1862, but the evidence against her was far from watertight. It was – and still is – strongly believed that the brutal killer was actually eighty-seven-year-old James Fleming, the father of the victim's employer. Under pressure, her execution was first postponed then cancelled altogether. When told of the commutation, she replied, 'Then I am to be kept in jail all my days?'

She was not kept in jail all her days, being released from Perth Prison in 1877. She remained in Scotland until her husband's death in 1880, then moved to America where she died in 1899. Seven years earlier, another woman, Isabella McGregor, claimed on her death bed that she had, in fact, murdered Miss McPherson but no corroborative evidence was produced.

By this time, the death penalty, with regard to women at least, was nearing the end of its rope although it remained on the statute books until finally being abolished in 1969. After the execution of baby-farmer Jessie King in 1889, it would be almost thirty-five years before a woman faced the noose again in Scotland. Her name was Susan Newell and she would be the first woman to hang in Glasgow since Helen Blackwood took part in her bizarre wedding ceremony facing Glasgow Green.

10

THE LAST DROP

Susan Newell, 1923

It was the biggest event the towns of Coatbridge and Airdrie had
seen for many a long year. The streets were thronged with people,
some fanning themselves against the heat of the summer's day.
Traffic was brought to a standstill as the procession passed through,
a band at its head and the children marching in close order behind.
It was quite a sight. It was a pity it marked such a sad occasion.
The death of a child – any child – is tragic but it is doubly so when
that child is taken from his or her parents in a violent fashion.

Young John Johnston was such a child. And, as his white-draped
coffin was lowered into its grave, one question hung in the summer
air as if plucked by the cool breeze from the minds and lips of all
present. The question swirled round the mourners and touched
the grieving parents and weeping sisters. It breathed among the
crowd gathered respectfully at the cemetery gates. It whispered to
the people still clogging the streets.

Why had this young boy's life been so cruelly cut short?

Why had this happened?

Why?

But only one person knew the answer and she was, at that
moment, in a prison cell a few miles away to the west. And she
was keeping her silence.

Susan Newell had not had much of a life. She was born in 1893
into a family of thirteen children. Poverty and hardship appeared
to be the bywords of her existence in which there was never
enough money and seldom any joy. She and her first husband did

have one child – little Janet McLeod. That must have made her happy momentarily until the reality that this was just another mouth to feed struck home.

The first marriage failed and she took up with another man, John Newell, a former soldier with the Scots Guards. But the daily grind of Susan's life had taken its toll on her temperament and she became quick to rile and swift with her fists. More than once she struck her new husband and this led to more arguments, more anger.

By 1923, the family was living in a rented room in the home of Mrs Annie Young in Newlands Road, Coatbridge, but the landlady was reaching the end of her tether regarding the almost constant rows. One June weekend, events reached a climax and the angry words and raised voices from the rented room tipped Mrs Young over the edge. She'd had enough, she told them. She wanted them to leave, she said. It was Sunday night and she agreed to let them stay until Monday but her mind was made up – they had to be gone by the Tuesday.

John Newell had also had enough. He stormed from the house, leaving his wife and stepdaughter behind. Later his fears of facing charges of wife desertion were replaced with something infinitely more terrifying – trial for capital murder.

John Johnstone was a bright boy of thirteen who regularly helped his friend, James McGhee, on his newspaper round. On Wednesday 20 June 1923, he rushed home from school to have his tea with his mother and then went out to meet James. A short time later, John took nine papers and trotted off to deliver them and collect money due.

Annie Young saw the young boy pushing open the Newell's door, which he did without knocking. She heard Susan Newell's sharp voice telling him to come in and shut the door. The young boy did as he was told.

No one knows for sure what happened inside the cramped little room. The only certainty is that this was the last time anyone other than Susan Newell saw John Johnstone alive.

Robert Johnstone, his father, returned home from work at around 5.10 p.m. for something to eat before he and his wife went off to attend the Coatbridge Cattle Show – something of a gala event and an attraction to more than just farmers. They came back at 9.15 p.m. to find that young John had not shown up. One of his daughters said that John had come in earlier but that he had then gone out again – she thought to the pictures. Mr Johnstone knew the picture show did not finish until 10.30 p.m. so he remained unconcerned and prepared for bed.

However, worry began to flutter in his mind by 11 p.m. when there was still no sign of the boy. He got up, dressed and went to the picture house which was, by then, in darkness. The father, growing more concerned with each step, walked the streets for an hour before reporting the boy's disappearance to the police. An officer said that young lads occasionally went back to the farms with the animals in the cattle show but inquiries at the showground proved fruitless. No one had seen the boy. It was an anguished Robert Johnstone who went home to spend a sleepless night – his mind filled with thoughts of his missing son.

The following day, with little else to do but wait, he went to work. That morning police contacted him and asked him to attend Glasgow's Eastern Police Headquarters. They had a body for him to identify. It was, of course, his son.

But who would want to kill such a young lad? And how had he ended up over 10 miles away in Glasgow? The answers prompted a trial judge to dub the case 'stranger than fiction'.

After she had seen the boy going into the Newell's room, Mrs Young had heard three strange noises. She called them 'dumps' but she thought nothing of them at the time. She was, after all, used to hearing loud noises from that particular room. Later that Wednesday night, Mrs Newell asked her landlady if she had a box and Mrs Young presumed it was to pack her personal belongings in before vacating the room. Mrs Young had no box, however, so Susan Newell turned and walked away. The landlady heard her go out and then return five or ten minutes later. Finally, at about 2.30 a.m., the woman heard Mrs Newell leave once again, this time with her young daughter in tow.

Six-year-old Janet had been playing in the street and had seen the paper boy going into the house but had not seen him come back out again afterwards. Later, her mother came out with an empty jug in her hand and told the little girl to come with her. They walked through the streets to Duff's Public House and Janet waited outside while Susan Newell went in. She came back with some whisky and the jug filled with beer. Then she took her daughter's hand and returned home.

The first thing Janet saw when she went into the room was the boy lying on the couch. Even at her tender years, she recognised a dead body when she saw one. Her mother told her to sit down and be quiet and Janet knew the woman's moods well enough to do as she was told. Susan sat in silence, drinking deeply from the jug of beer and the bottle of whisky and staring at the corpse, at the blood now caking on his head, at the eyes dull and lifeless. She did not like seeing his dead face so she covered it with a pair of her husband's underpants.

As she drank, she pondered the problem that has faced murderers since the beginning of time – what to do with the body. She used a poker to try to prise up the floorboards but they were nailed down too tightly. Then she went across the landing to ask Mrs Young for a box. Finally, she decided to move the corpse out of the room altogether. Out of the street. In fact, out of the town.

There was an old go-kart under the bed so she hauled it out and wrapped the little body in a bed sheet. Then, in the early hours of the morning when the streets were quiet and deserted, she trundled it out of the house and headed off down the road with her six-year-old daughter perched on top of the grisly bundle.

Susan Newell hauled the corpse to Glasgow Road where the kart developed a fault and she had trouble manoeuvring it. The sky was beginning to lighten and a woman offered to give her a hand but she politely turned it down. Then a lorry coughed to a halt beside them and the driver, the magnificently moustached Thomas Dickson, offered his assistance. Susan Newell explained she was going to Glasgow to look for rooms to rent. As luck would have it, Mr Dickson was heading to Glasgow to pick up a load and would be glad to give them a lift.

Susan Newell thought about this for a second, then thanked him and said he could drop them off anywhere. Refusing any help, she hefted the go-kart on to the back and then she and her daughter climbed into the cab. Dickson took them down Edinburgh Road into Glasgow's east end. At the corner of Netherfield Street and Duke Street, he stopped and was thanked for his kindness. Again he offered to help drag the kart down from the truck but the woman was adamant that she could manage.

However, although she had been able to hoist the kart on to the truck, taking it back off again proved more difficult. As she pulled at it, her bundle toppled and Dickson reached out to steady it. Panicking, Mrs Newell angrily slapped his hand away. No doubt peeved at the way he had been treated when all he was doing was being a good Samaritan, the lorry driver drove away, completely unaware that he had been helping a killer dispose of a body.

But Susan Newell's luck had run out. As the bundle fell, the bed sheet slipped and John Johnstone's foot was revealed. Dickson had not noticed it but someone else, who just happened to be looking out of her window at that particular moment, had spotted it. And, as Susan Newell rearranged the cover, sharp-eyed Mrs Helen Elliot, standing at her window at 802 Duke Street, caught a glimpse of a child's head.

This wasn't right. This wasn't right at all.

The woman charged out into the landing of the tenement and battered on the door of her neighbours. She told them what she had seen and asked them to keep an eye on the woman and child in the street while she ran to fetch the police.

Susan Newell, the body now again fully covered, had thrown the bundle over her shoulder and left Janet to handle the near-useless go-kart. She was heading towards the city and a 'coup', or dump, where she had planned to leave the corpse. There was little thought of what would happen after that, little thought of the witnesses she had left behind – although she had already primed the little witness wheeling the go-kart at her side. However, she only managed to reach the mouth of the close at 850 Duke Street before the dead weight over her shoulder took its toll. This will do, she decided, and stepped into the tenement building.

As she disappeared into the gloom of the close mouth, witnesses stopped a police officer on patrol and told him there was a woman in number 850 with what looked like a dead body in a bag. The policeman stopped Susan Newell when she emerged from the close and took her back inside. Lying on the cold stone floor to the rear of the ground-floor corridor he found John Johnstone's body, still wrapped in the bed sheet.

Susan Newell had her story all ready. 'My husband did that,' she said.

Under questioning at the police station, she said that she and John Newell had been quarrelling when the paperboy came in the door. The lad had cried out when he had seen her husband raising a fist to strike her so John Newell had grabbed the boy to shut him up, throwing him on the bed. And there he choked the life out of him.

Mrs Newell said that she had fainted at that point but, when she had come round, her man was gone and the boy lay dead on the bed. In a state of shock, she had fed her own daughter and then they had wheeled the body to Glasgow. It was all to protect her husband, she said. Ask my daughter.

So they did – and little Janet confirmed everything.

The only problem was John Newell hadn't been in the room at the time that John Johnstone had been murdered. But that tiny little fact didn't stop the police from charging him with the killing when they caught up with him – and nor did it prevent the procurator fiscal from later pursuing a capital murder charge against him. Ex-soldier John Newell had three months of hell ahead of him for something he did not do.

x x x

On 25 June, young John Johnstone was buried in New Monkland Cemetery. The procession began in his home in Coatbridge's Whifflet Street and followed roads through the town and neighbouring Airdrie to the graveyard.

He had been a popular lad. Friends from his Boys' Brigade company attended in full uniform, as did children from the Boy Scouts, the Girl Guides and pupils from his school. The memorial stone to be placed at the head of his grave simply read, 'In memory of John Johnstone from his playmates.'

As the procession left the family home, things proved too much for one of his sisters, May, who collapsed and had to be helped back inside. It was not the only display of emotion that day, as many of the women among the thousands who lined the streets wept openly. Shops along the route closed as the cortège marched past to the slow beat of the Salvation Army band at its head and window blinds were drawn as a mark of sadness over the loss of an innocent.

On the same day, a Monday, the Newells appeared at Glasgow Sheriff Court to be charged with the boy's murder. The indictment read that they had beaten him on the head with a blunt instrument, throttled him and broken his neck. It emerged later that the left side of his head had also been burned. An expert witness believed that his face had been held against a lit gas ring. The obviously nervous twenty-nine-year-old Susan Newell pleaded not guilty while her husband lodged a special defence of alibi. However, this was only a formal appearance and the real drama would take place in September.

A public, hungry for details of what had become known as the 'go-kart murder', began queuing up outside Glasgow's High Court of Justiciary at 4 a.m. on the morning of Tuesday 18 September 1923. By the time the doors opened at 9 a.m., over 1000 people were standing in the Saltmarket but only 100 of them could get in. The rest had to gather in the street, impatiently awaiting news from inside the courtroom. That impatience boiled over when the two accused were driven up to the gates. The crowd surged around the police van, eager for a glimpse of the arch-villains, and were held back by a small army of police officers.

Seventy witnesses had been called and forty of them were heard on the first day. Among them was the dead boy's mother, still in her mourning black. During her testimony, the emotion of talking about her little boy's final hours and the prospect of handling his jersey proved too much and the proceedings had to be halted to give her time to recover. All the while, ashen-faced Susan Newell craned forward in the dock, watching and listening intently.

But, out of all the evidence given by witnesses that day, the most forceful and most damaging was that of little Janet McLeod. She was crying softly as she was led into the court and seated on a chair, a woman officer standing by her side to comfort her. Originally, she had told police that her stepfather had killed the 'wee laddie' but, in court, she admitted she only said that because her mammie had told her to. Her stepfather had not been there, she said.

Hesitantly, the young girl told the court about her mammie calling her in and her seeing the little dead boy on the couch; of the walking trip to Glasgow; of getting 'a hurl' on the go-kart on top of the dead boy. All the while, Susan Newell listened to her daughter verbally signing her death warrant, her eyes darting backwards and forwards but otherwise her face emotionless. The only time a trace of emotion crossed her face was when her counsel described the trip to Glasgow with her daughter sitting on the go-kart. As he talked, Mrs Newell wiped away a few tears that welled up in her eyes.

Finally, John Newell's ordeal came to an end. There was no evidence to link him in any way to the murder – in fact, he had provided a very detailed alibi for his movements on the day John Johnstone had died. After he had left the rented room following their most recent argument, Newell had attended his brother's funeral on the Tuesday and stayed for a while at his father's house. He had then spent the night in a lodging house, in the

Pollok area of Glasgow, before travelling to the east end of the city where, on the Wednesday night, he had gone to a show in a music hall. A barman there recalled undercharging him for a round of drinks. He had then visited his sister and finally felt he should report to a police station to see if he was wanted for wife desertion. On being told he was not, he had taken a room at another lodging house and, on the Thursday, hitched a lift to Leith and then on to Haddington. It was while he was there that he had read in the newspapers about the murder and handed himself in to the local police. The police and the procurator fiscal had known of this alibi from the very beginning and everything he had told them would have been easy to check but they had proceeded with the murder charge against him regardless.

On the second and last day of the trial, the charges against John Newell were finally dropped and he was able to walk from the dock a free man. He walked away from the woman he must have once loved without a glance. She, however, never took her eyes off him.

There was no question that Susan McAllister Newell had murdered the boy. The only question was over her state of mind at the time. If it could be proved that she was insane, she could escape the hangman. However, despite valiant attempts by her defence counsel to prove otherwise, a succession of medical witnesses testified that she was mentally competent. They found her cool, certainly, but she answered their questions easily. One damned her as being of the 'tinker class' and having a 'want of moral fibre'. But she was sane, he said.

The legendary Professor John Glaister, Chair of Forensic Medicine at the University of Glasgow, had also examined her. He had no doubts about the soundness of her mind although he allowed that she was not of 'high intelligence' and he could not rule out the possibility of temporary insanity at the time of the murder. However, it was reckoned that she understood the severity of the charge against her – the very fact that she had tried to cover up the killing showed that she could tell right from wrong – and so the plea of insanity was not accepted. In the end, the all-male jury took only thirty-five minutes to reach a majority verdict of guilty but added a unanimous recommendation for mercy.

The presiding judge, Lord Alness, had some words to say before passing judgement.

> The story which has been unfolded to us during these two days is a pathetic and even a poignant one. Moreover, it is a strange story.
>
> The sequel to this boy's death, however it occurred, is such that if a novelist wrote it, probably a lasting public judgement would pronounce it quite incredible. But, as we know, truth is often stranger than fiction.

Despite the jury's plea for mercy, the judge had no option but to pronounce the severest penalty of the law on the woman for her crime. Draping the black cap on his head, he sentenced her to be hanged on 10 October.

The condemned woman took the news as coolly as she had taken most of the evidence during her trial. She rose when her name was called and stood perfectly still as the judge made his speech and pronounced her doom. Finally, she turned away smartly and was led to the cells below.

Outside, the restless crowd learned of the sentence and tried to rush the gates as she was led into a van to be taken back to her cell at Duke Street Prison. The authorities had learned their lesson from the disorder of the previous day. A small army of police officers had been drafted into the Saltmarket and moved quickly to hold the rabble back. However, the shouting and catcalls from the frustrated mob could still be heard inside the courtroom.

There had not been a woman hanged in Scotland for almost thirty-four years – seventy in Glasgow – although in 1922 husband and wife Willie and Helen Harkness had been due to die for the brutal murder of Elizabeth Benjamin in Glasgow's Whiteinch area. A few days prior to the execution Mrs Harkness had had her sentence commuted to life imprisonment but her husband had not been so fortunate – he was hanged in the January. The jury had recommended mercy towards Susan Newell and there were moves to have her death sentence quashed. However, the Secretary of State for Scotland decided there could be no such reprieve for the go-kart killer and ordered that her execution proceed as planned. When the condemned woman was given this news, she cried out and shed tears for her daughter. It was her first real display of emotion since the horror began.

On a bleak 10 October 1923, Susan Newell was led from the condemned cell of Duke Street Prison into the execution room. Two Roman Catholic priests accompanied her, murmuring words of comfort. Her pace was steady, her gaze unwavering and she seemed to have recovered the 'unnatural calm' observed by reporters during the trial. As he fumbled with the rope, the hangman, Walter Ellis, showed more nerves than she did. He was never comfortable with hanging women and it is said that this contributed greatly to the deterioration of mind that led to him committing suicide some years later. He had his assistant strap her legs and thighs to prevent her skirts from flapping upwards when he pulled the lever but the experienced hangman failed to tie her wrists properly. Mrs Newell reacted only once to the procedure. When Ellis tried to cover her face with the customary hood, she pulled her hands free and objected, 'Don't put that thing over my head!' Ellis agreed to do without it and instantly opened the drop. The lack of a hood meant the witnessing authorities saw her face as she died.

Susan Newell was the last woman to be hanged in Scotland and the only one to have been executed in Duke Street Prison, which no longer exists (blocks of flats were built on the site near to Glasgow Cathedral and legend has it that ghosts were said to haunt the area for decades afterwards). Walter Ellis said that she died bravely and she was the bravest woman he had ever dropped.

She also died without ever saying what happened in that rented room in June. Why had she suddenly snapped and killed an innocent lad? Had her husband's desertion and her imminent homelessness caused temporary insanity? Did the boy say the wrong thing? Did he, as some writers have suggested, simply ask for payment, and did that tip her over the edge?

We shall never know. But eleven years later another Scotswoman found herself facing the gallows, again for child murder. And, like Susan Newell, she told no one what happened.

11

SACKCLOTH AND ASHES

Jeannie Donald, 1934

The rain had been beating down steadily for some time, slicking the city streets and filling the gutters, the drops reflecting the flashes of the torches as they searched. The sound of raised voices floated through the downpour; men's voices and women's voices, each calling a name – a girl's name. They had been hunting since early evening, looking for a little girl lost, an innocent abroad in the city. But there was no sign of her, no trace of the eight-year-old who had gone missing at lunchtime.

By midnight, the hunting parties decided to call a halt and resume again at first light. The girl's father, though, refused to give up, refused to give in. He would carry on, he said, until they found his wee lassie. But, by two in the morning the futility of it all penetrated his body with the tears of rain and he decided to go home. He would look again as soon as dawn broke. He would keep looking. Had to keep looking. And hopefully she would be found and everything would be all right again.

But there was to be no happy ending to this story. The little girl was found but she was dead – bundled into a sack and dumped near to her own front door. First impressions suggested she had been sexually assaulted and then murdered. First impressions, though, can so often be wrong.

Helen Priestly was last seen alive in the street near her tenement home, in Aberdeen's Urquhart Road, at lunchtime on Friday 20 April 1934. Her mother, Agnes, had sent the girl to the local Co-op for a loaf of bread before she was due to return to school.

Five-year-old Jane Yule spotted Helen making her way home with the purchase. After that, there was no sign of the eight-year-old for fifteen hours – until her body was discovered the following morning.

Her father, painter and decorator, John Priestly, came home later that day to find his wife distraught. Helen had disappeared, Agnes told him. She had checked with the school but their daughter had not returned to class after lunch. And so the searches began, lasting all through the night in that cold early spring rainstorm.

Fears were heightened when a local lad told police that he had seen Helen being taken away by a man. There had been a child abduction a few weeks earlier and the description that the boy gave – a middle-aged man in a long coat with a rip in the back – fitted the suspect in the previous case. Hours later, though, the boy admitted he had made the whole thing up.

At two the next morning, John Priestly sat in the warm kitchen of his friend, Alexander Parker, who lived across the road. The anguished father was talked into getting some rest and Mr Parker promised to fetch him before dawn to go out again.

At just before five, unaware that his friend had already left the house, Alexander Parker made his way across the road to the Priestly's tenement. On his way to the stairs leading to the family's first-floor flat, he noticed a sack shoved into a recess near to the ground-floor communal toilet. He moved closer in the gloom and saw a child's foot protruding from it. Peeking inside, he recognised the body of young Helen.

The news spread swiftly through the four-storey tenement and people came out on to the various landings to see what was going on. Only the tenants of the two flats on the ground floor failed to respond. A William Topp and his wife occupied one. Mr Topp had been part of the search the night before and had already left to begin again. His pregnant wife was so startled by the screams and shouts outside that she collapsed and subsequently miscarried.

Alexander Donald and his wife, Jeannie, rented the other flat. According to Mrs Donald, her husband prevented her from investigating the noise by saying that there was nothing they could do. The family had not been involved in the search for the missing girl as there was, reportedly, no love lost between them and the Priestlys.

Agnes Priestly was naturally devastated by the discovery, as Mr Parker said later. 'Mrs Priestly came running down the stairs, crying "Oh, my bairn! Oh, my bairn!" and made to lift Helen into her arms but I stopped her and assisted her upstairs to the house.'

Jeannie Donald later stated she heard someone cry out, 'She's been used!' but this was never confirmed.

But little Helen had been used and used badly. The newspapers of the time delicately described her as having been 'outraged' but, nowadays, they would call it what it at least appeared to be – sexual assault. And a brutal one at that.

The youngster had bruises around her throat which suggested strangulation. However, particles of vomit were later found lodged in her throat and these could have caused death by asphyxiation. There was more vomit on her clothes and blood caked on her legs and thighs. The area around her vagina was seriously injured and it appeared as if her killer had violently abused her.

From the start, detectives believed she knew her killer. Helen was a tall lass for her age but she was shy and unlikely to go anywhere with a stranger. She had apparently vanished from a densely populated street, at a busy time of day, yet no one had seen her being taken. Also, the child's body and the sack in which she was found were dry. Considering the heavy rain since the previous night, this suggested that the killer was someone from inside the building. So police concentrated their efforts on the eight flats in the tenement – in particular, given the presumed sex attack, the comings and goings of the men.

The body was found lying on its right side but evidence of lividity – the post-mortem settling of blood – could be seen on the dead girl's left side. This could have meant that Helen had been kept somewhere else after death and then moved to this spot.

They had a rough timescale to work on. The ground-floor toilets and the area around the rear door to the building had been searched late on the previous night. The sack had not been there at 1.30 a.m. when Mr Topp had gone out to use the toilet. The girl's father had not noticed it when he had left the building at around 4.30 a.m. to scour the streets in daylight. Whoever had dumped the sack did so just minutes before Mr Parker arrived.

Once the pathologists got to work on the little body, police also had a rough time of death. A study of the girl's stomach contents revealed that she had died within an hour or two of eating her lunch. That placed the murder at approximately 2 p.m. or even earlier. This created a problem. Every man in the building had an alibi for around that time – they were all at work and with witnesses to prove it. But the girl had been brutally raped – the wounds on her vagina proved that – so it had to be a man they were looking for.

Again, the pathologists stepped in. Certainly, the injuries had been inflicted before death but by something like a poker or a broom handle. Whoever had done this wanted to give the impression of rape. This discovery changed everything. The killer need not have been a man. In fact, it was more likely to have been a woman trying to deflect suspicion away from herself. But who would do such a terrible thing? And why?

Because the family did not want the sad event turned into a circus, Helen was buried in a simple but secret ceremony in the city's Allenvale Cemetery on Wednesday 25 April. The police investigation had expanded from the tenement although they still believed their quarry lived there. Meanwhile, word of the killing flowed like the rain across the city and parents grew worried that a sex killer was on the loose. Children were accompanied to and from school, even if the journey was a short one. After all, Helen had only gone a few hundred yards down the street to the shop.

One line of inquiry centred on the bag in which the body had been found. The canvas flour sack had the word 'BOSS' written on it in 5-inch high red letters and was supplied by the Lukena

Milling Company of Atchison, Kansas, reaching Britain through a Canadian mill. Filled with cereals, the sacks were shipped to London and then to Glasgow before arriving in Aberdeen. After that, the empty sacks were dispersed to who knew where although one grocer, interviewed as part of the investigation, recalled giving a sack to a 'woman of the poorer classes' but he did not remember it having any distinguishing marks. Closer inspection revealed a hole in one corner, where it had perhaps been hung on a hook. There were traces of cinders in the sack and these seemed to match the cinders that had been found on the girl's body. Human hairs were also found clinging to the cloth which did not match those of the murdered child.

But, on the day of Helen's funeral, police zeroed in on their suspects. Despite interviewing hundreds of people in the four days since the murder had been discovered, detectives remained convinced that the killer lived in the tenement. Their prime suspects were the Donald family. It was well known they had little time for the Priestlys although the precise reason for this appeared to be buried in the past. For their part, the Priestlys said they tried to be civil, although little Helen often called Mrs Donald 'Coconut' which did not endear her to the woman. It was also revealed that Helen was in the habit of 'chapping' on the Donald's door and then running away.

In his account of the case, leading forensic scientist, Sir Sydney Smith – who was, at that time, Chair of Forensic Medicine at Edinburgh University – described the Donalds as 'dour and taciturn'. He did, however, opine that Mrs Donald was 'a good looking woman' who was a regular church-goer and who attended weekly meetings of the Salvation Army. Her husband, Alexander, was a hairdresser. Their daughter, also called Jeannie, was a school friend of Helen Priestly. The two girls apparently did not share their parent's enmity but, on one occasion, young Jeannie had hit the younger Helen and had been told off by Mrs Priestly.

At 11 a.m. on the morning of the funeral, the police came calling once again at the Donald's door. They had further questions to ask and some searching to do. Jeannie Donald willingly let them in and agreed to the search. As officers combed the small flat, she was asked once more to account for her movements on the day Helen had disappeared.

Young Jeannie was a talented dancer, Mrs Donald told them, and she had spent most of the afternoon ironing five dresses for Jeannie's rehearsal that evening. The police asked if she could be more specific about the time she spent ironing and, with her hands tapping the table top to some secret beat, she said it had been from about 2.15 until 4.00. She said that, just after she had finished ironing, young Jeannie had come home and, having had their tea, they had set off for the rehearsal at the Beach Pavilion. Her husband had come to pick them up and all three had arrived home just after eleven at night.

The police asked Mrs Donald when she had first heard about Helen's disappearance. Mrs Donald told them that it had not been until around four, after she had finished the ironing. She had been out earlier in the day – firstly at the market on The Green and later she had looked at some dress material.

They then enquired about the time she had come back. She said it had been just after two o'clock. She told them that she had been out for around an hour and that, on her return, she had noticed a lot of people at the corner, including a tearful Mrs Priestly.

Next they asked if anyone could corroborate the time of her return and she said she had spoken to her neighbour, Mrs Topp, before going into her own flat to begin her ironing.

The police were with Mrs Donald for thirteen hours. Her husband came home for his lunch and was kept there for questioning. Only their daughter was allowed to return to school in the afternoon.

Officers found little of evidentiary value in the house – apart from some curious stains on the floor of a cupboard. Dr Richards, the city's police surgeon and a lecturer in forensic science, made a preliminary check and declared the stains to be blood but he said he would have to conduct more stringent tests in his laboratory. Neither Mr nor Mrs Donald were able to explain how the stains got there. They both denied being involved in any way with Helen's death but the investigating officers felt they had enough to charge the couple with the murder.

Locals were aware that the police had been in the flat for a long time and, in the street, a hostile crowd had gathered around the paddy wagon. Uniformed police forced the press of people back to allow detectives to escort the suspects into the back of the van. They then had to clear the road so that the van could leave and make its way to Police Headquarters in Castle Street.

However, the murder of a child generates strong feelings and word that arrests had been made in connection with Helen Priestly's killing soon echoed across the city. When the van arrived at police HQ, another crowd of around 2000 people had gathered. Again, officers held the furious and screaming mob back while the man and woman were shepherded swiftly inside.

Feelings ran just as high on 4 May when hundreds of people milled around outside Aberdeen's Sheriff Court. The Donalds appeared there – in private and so away from the accusing eyes of the public – to be formally charged with assaulting Helen Wilson Robertson Priestly by seizing her, holding her, compressing her throat, cutting or stabbing her and murdering her. However, just over one month later, Alexander Donald was freed. During his six weeks in custody, police had unsuccessfully tried to break his alibi that he was at work and so were forced to concede that the man was innocent of the murder.

That left only thirty-eight-year-old Jeannie Donald in the shadow of the gallows.

Mrs Donald's own alibi did not stand up to much scrutiny. Inquiries at the street market at which she claimed to have bought some groceries revealed the prices she'd quoted were from the previous week. Similarly, the shop where she'd looked at the fabric had been closed on the Friday afternoon in question. Police suspected the shopping trip the accused had described had taken place the week before.

She could certainly have seen the crowd on the corner and Mrs Priestly crying – but from her own window. Mrs Topp confirmed that she had seen Mrs Donald that afternoon in the lobby but she had been standing at the main entrance and it was a good fifteen minutes later than Mrs Donald had said.

During the search of the flat, police found sacks hanging on hooks with holes in the corners similar to the one that had acted as little Helen's shroud. But none of them had 'BOSS' on the front. Moreover, on further examination, the suspicious stains on the cupboard floor proved not to be blood at all. However, tests made on stains on other items in the house – washing cloths, newspapers, a scrubbing brush and a segment of linoleum – did prove positive for blood. Helen had been Group O and the blood found on these items were also Group O. Similarly, bacteria on one of the washing cloths was also found to be of the same type found in Helen's blood, due to a rupture of the child's intestinal canal which had possibly happened during the feigned rape.

Hairs and household fluff found in the sack were compared to samples from the Donald house. The human hairs were examined closely and bore what was described as a 'striking resemblance' to those of Jeannie Donald, samples of which had been obtained from a hairbrush she had used while in prison. The household fluff also matched similar samples taken from the Donald house, and scientists – led by Sir Sydney Smith – decided that the particular combination of materials found was only evident in the Donald home. Samples from other houses in the tenement had been examined but had been found not to match. Studies of the cinders discovered in the sack and on Helen's body proved inconclusive but the remains of a loaf of bread were also taken from the Donald home. This was the kind of bread that Helen Priestly had bought and, according to young Jeannie, was not the same type usually eaten at the Donald table.

Due to the intense public interest in the case, the trial was heard, not in the Granite City, but at Edinburgh's High Court, beginning on Monday 16 July 1934. The Crown proposed to lead 164 witnesses, including young Jeannie. There were 202 productions listed on the indictment, many of them linked to the all-important scientific evidence uncovered by Sir Sidney Smith's team. Professor John Glaister, Chair of Forensic Medicine at the University of Glasgow and an expert in the study of hair, was part of the team as well. He had also been involved in the Susan Newell case (*see* p. 154).

What none of the witnesses or experts could provide was a reason for Mrs Donald killing little Helen. The accused remained tight-lipped although she continued to deny the charge. She did not give evidence in her defence. Her team concentrated on trying to discredit the scientific evidence levelled by the crown. They insisted the findings were inconclusive and continually pointed to the lack of motive. Of course, there is no need to provide a motive under law, just the evidence that proves guilt to the satisfaction of the jury.

In his summing up for the jury, the judge, Lord Aitchison, said, 'To your mind, to my mind, no motive could ever be adequate for taking the life of a child,' and he added, 'There are some crimes which are committed in darkness and gloom. This was one. When this foul thing was done there were only two persons present – the murderer and the victim.'

On the fifth and last day of the trial, the jury of ten men and five women took only eighteen minutes to reach their verdict. Jeannie Donald stood in the dock – eyes fixed straight ahead as the foreman stood to read out the decision. When the word 'Guilty' boomed out, she groaned and slumped to the side and only her police escort prevented her from falling. The despair that plaintive moan carried caused tears to well in the eyes of jury members and court observers.

Lord Aitchison cleaned and recleaned his glasses as the verdict was recorded. He had never passed the death sentence on anyone during his years on the bench and the fact that his first was a woman made it doubly difficult. Fixing his glasses on his nose, he stared at the accused from the bench and placed the black cap on his head. Jeannie Donald was to be taken from that place and kept in custody until Monday 13 August, when she was to be hanged by the neck until dead – the first woman to die on the gallows since Susan Newell in Glasgow eleven years ago.

Mrs Donald's lawyers lodged an appeal on 3 August. The wheels of justice grind notoriously slowly – when they grind at all – but they expected to have some sort of news within two weeks. But, the day after lodging the papers, Aberdeen's Lord Provost, Mr Henry Alexander, was required to cut short a holiday in Ballater to visit Craiginches Prison. There he met Jeannie Donald in her cell and read a letter from the Secretary of State for Scotland. It read:

> With reference to the case of Jeannie Ewen or Donald, now being under sentence of death in His Majesty's Prison, Aberdeen, I have to inform you that, after full consideration, I have felt justified in advising His Majesty to respite execution of the capital sentence with a view to its committal to penal servitude for life.

It must have been a much-relieved Jeannie Donald who thanked the Lord Provost and then sank on to her bed. Ten days later she walked a mile from Craiginches to Aberdeen's railway station, accompanied by two prison guards, and boarded a train for Glasgow. She was to serve her sentence – which, in the end, lasted only ten years – at Duke Street Prison, the same prison where Susan Newell had walked to her death. The prisoner and her escort were in civilian dress and no one recognised the person who, only a few short weeks before, had been the most hated woman in the city.

Many commentators on the case, including Sir Sydney Smith, believed that she had never intended murder. What she did had been an attempt to chastise the girl for some upset and it had gone tragically wrong. During the post-mortem, pathologists discovered that Helen Priestly suffered from an enlarged thymus – a gland that should grow until the child is two years of age and then slowly reduce. But Helen's gland had not shrunk as it should have and it might have placed pressure on her heart. In the opinion of some medical men, this would leave the child susceptible to fainting or even death, should she receive a sudden shock.

So, let us assume that Helen, on her way upstairs with her loaf of bread from the Co-op, decides to bang on Mrs Donald's door and gallop away up to her flat. Let us also assume that Mrs Donald sees her coming and lies in wait – grabbing the girl, perhaps from behind. The sudden shock causes the youngster to lose consciousness, leading the woman to panic, thinking the child is dead. She drags the body into her house where she simulates the rape with some household implement (although no evidence was found in the house to support this). But, as the implement is being inserted into her vagina, the girl comes to life, perhaps brought round by the extreme pain. She screams – a scream heard by a slater working nearby but by no one else. Helen vomits and some of the matter catches in her throat. Mrs Donald's panic heightens and she wraps her fingers round the girl's throat to quieten her, squeezing tighter and tighter until the screaming stops, the struggling ceases and the girl lies lifeless on the linoleum.

She hides the body in a cinder box under the kitchen sink. Later examinations revealed no cinder box but marks of where it had once rested were clearly seen and it was assumed it had been destroyed because it was saturated with blood from the girl's horrific wounds. With the body out of sight, Mrs Donald goes about her business – ironing the dresses, feeding her daughter, taking her to the dance rehearsal. She also washes away what blood she can see. But blood will out, as she was to discover, and microscopic traces are found on the various household items taken away for examination. Then, during the early hours of the following morn-ing, Helen is bundled into the sack – taking the cinders, household fluff and hairs with her – and dumped in the hallway.

But all this is mere supposition. Like Susan Newell before her, only the victim and her murderer knew what really happened in that cramped tenement hallway that Friday lunchtime. Helen

Priestly never had the chance to tell. Jeannie Donald, although luckier than Susan Newell, also took her secret to the grave.

12

ACT OF MADNESS

Jean Waddell, 1961

The children had been playing in the street when the woman approached them. They knew her for, thanks to her eccentric behaviour, few people in the street did not. But she seemed so nice as she invited them up to her top-floor flat.

Minutes later, out of the seven youngsters who had climbed those Glasgow tenement stairs with the woman, four lay seriously injured on the pavement with a fifth, a four-year-old girl, dead. The woman who had been so nice had suddenly turned on them and tossed them – almost carelessly – from the window to plunge 40 feet on to the cold and uncaring concrete below. The sixth and seventh children managed to escape when a neighbour, alerted by the children's screams, kicked in the door.

The city reeled in shock as it learned of the diabolical incident. Its citizens came to realise that the system, designed to protect them from such things, had completely failed them. For, although the act she had committed was evil, the woman herself was not. She was a sick and tormented individual who could not cope with her ever-growing madness and had been all but deserted by a profession that believed she was responding to treatment. In fact, her fractured mind was not responding to treatment but she knew she would rather die than go back to an institution. And so she hatched a desperate plan that she believed would take her to the gallows.

But, for the children – the innocent victims in a game of madness and fear – the whys and wherefores of her actions were immaterial. The survivors would never forget the ordeal of those few minutes in that cramped Glasgow flat, nor the playmate who was not as lucky as they had been. They had not done anything wrong. They had not tormented the woman in any way. All they had wanted was to see the puppies . . .

Jean Barclay Waddell first displayed signs of the madness that took her down the road to murder while in Canada. On 15 May 1945 – eight days after the end of the war in Europe – she married Canadian soldier Floyd Oakman following a wartime romance. He had actually met her sister first but, as she was already engaged, he found himself drawn to Jean. For two years they wrote to each other until deciding to become man and wife when he was on leave. However, the marriage was not to last. They had only three days together before they split up. Her new husband rejoined his unit in London and she returned to her parents' house in Ruther-glen. Finally, in 1946, they decided to try again and so twenty-two-year-old Jean sailed off to join Mr Oakman on his family farm in the Canadian prairie province of Saskatchewan.

But wedded bliss was not to be for the young couple. Six weeks after she arrived at the remote farm, Jean walked out and filed for divorce. The mental changes that were to turn her into a murderer were beginning to take shape. Floyd later said she had become a different person, her moods changing in a moment.

It was not her sanity that brought her to the attention of the medical authorities but a resurgence of tuberculosis, then a fairly common – if serious – lung complaint. She had first fought the disease as a teenager but now it was back and she spent two years in a Canadian sanatorium before being discharged. However, TB can be a tenacious condition and it soon flared up yet again, forcing her to be admitted to yet another hospital. Here, for reasons clear only to her own increasingly fevered mind, she was convinced someone was trying to murder her. One night she snapped and attacked a nurse. The authorities promptly sent her to a mental institution.

In 1950, her brother John emigrated to Canada and tracked his sister down to Wayburn Mental Institution in Saskatchewan. He managed to convince the authorities that it would be best if Jean was released into his care and promised to take her back to Scotland and the security of their parents' home. She would be loved there. She would be safe there.

So, after four years away, Jean Waddell made the trip back across the Atlantic to her childhood home. Confined to the house, she continued to exhibit sharp mood swings. One moment she would be smiling and friendly, the next moody and uncommunicative. Strange, dark obsessions preyed on her mind and she became suspicious and resentful.

But, despite these lightning-fast changes of mood, she displayed a fiercely independent spirit and a desire to strike out on her own. Finally, she established a chicken farm near Dunoon but, as she had no real head for business, the enterprise failed and she found herself back with her loving family in Rutherglen.

And the madness grew. Dressed in old army jerkins and baggy slacks, she would leave home, hitching lifts on lorries to various parts of the country. That stopped when she was found penniless, hungry and living in a tent in the Lake District. A good Samaritan wrote to inform her mother of her plight and, once again, Jean had to be brought home to Glasgow. Her restless spirit and troubled mind prevented her from finding any real continuity in life, despite taking a number of decent jobs – including work as a shorthand typist and hotel receptionist and even trying her hand at nursing.

Finally, she bought her own flat at 39 Toryglen Street, Oatlands, in Glasgow, for £150. Her family was unhappy at the thought of her living alone – they even went to the extent of trying to prevent the sale. However, Jean was determined to make her own way.

But, almost as soon as she moved into this home of her own, her demons came raging back and she began to deteriorate. At first, it was rats that obsessed her. She became convinced that the tenement was infested with the creatures. She could hear them scurrying about in unseen corners, she said, and scrambling behind skirting-boards. She blamed her neighbours for the infestation, accusing them of encouraging the vermin and this, naturally, led to several arguments.

Her mania began to look outwith her immediate environment for expression and focused on a house in Polmadie Road which, she was convinced, was being used as a brothel. She told police officers that the prostitutes operating there hung from the windows and screamed abuse at her.

Even the police were not immune from her growing paranoia and soon she launched an ambitious letter-writing campaign, denouncing officers as pimps and even murderers. Among the recipients was the Chief Constable of the City of Glasgow, not to mention newspapers, the Secretary of State for Scotland and even Prime Minister Harold MacMillan. Finally, the police could take no more and Jean was dragged away to be examined by a psychiatrist, who admitted her to Hawkhead Mental Hospital where she was subjected to rigorous electro-convulsive treatment (ECT). This controversial procedure had been in use since the 1930s and involves the patient receiving electric shocks to the brain in order to provoke convulsions and stimulate the creation of antidepressant neurotransmitters. And four weeks later doctors decided that she was responding well to the therapy – well enough to be released. So, Jean Waddell, by then thirty-seven years of age, returned to her one-roomed flat. But now she had a new terror. She never wanted to return to hospital.

There then followed fifty-five days of growing instability. In addition to the fear of going back to an institution, she began to worry about conceiving an illegitimate child following a solitary bout of sex with an acquaintance. In desperation, she tried to kill herself by swallowing a box of aspirin. But she lost her nerve, staggered down the tenement stairs to a public phone box and dialled 999. She was rushed by ambulance to Glasgow Royal Infirmary where she was treated for two days before being sent to the psychiatric wing of Duke Street Hospital. She stayed there for a further two days before, once again, being allowed home. But she was not cured. Her terrors had increased after the abortive suicide attempt. She thought the police had heard about what she had done and were keeping her under surveillance. She imagined detectives were dogging her every move.

On Tuesday 28 March 1961, she was in the city centre thinking about buying an air pistol to shoot herself. Although she decided against this because she believed the shopkeeper would alert the police, she remained dead set against ever facing doctors again. With this thought nagging away at her, she went home to Oatlands. By then she had murder in mind.

At just after 6.00 p.m., fifty-four-year-old James Hainey was in his ground-floor flat having his tea when he heard a scream. He looked towards his window just as a child's body flashed past. Running out of the tenement close into the street, he saw a child lying on the pavement. Instinctively, he looked up, only to see a young boy being thrown from the top-floor window – the little body flailing towards him. He tried to catch the youngster but there was nothing he could do . . .

Meanwhile, thirty-two-year-old railway worker George Sutherland was leaning from his flat, preparing to wash the windows, when he glanced down and saw the bodies of three young children spread-eagled on the ground. At first he could not comprehend what had happened – until he saw a young girl clinging desperately to the window of the flat next door. Then she lost her precarious grip and plunged the 40 feet to the street . . .

A few doors away, Mrs May Lennon wondered where her son and daughter were. Five minutes earlier, she had sent five-year-old Margaret to fetch her older brother, Frankie, aged seven, for his tea. She went out into the street and looked along the road. Four closes away she could see three children lying on the ground – and a fourth plummeting from a window. She cried out and darted along the road, closely followed by her husband Tom . . .

By this time, George Sutherland had dashed from his flat and kicked open the door to his neighbour's flat – Jean Waddell's door.

As the wood splintered and the door flew open, a young boy of eight rushed out screaming.

He was too late to save the five children who had been pitched out of the window. Their crushed and bloody bodies lay on the pavement below. Margaret and Frankie Lennon were barely conscious, suffering from various broken bones. Four-year-old Thomas Devaney also had a number of fractures. Five-year-old Daniel McNeill had head injuries and was in a bad way. He would, however, eventually pull through. But poor little Marjorie Hughes, aged four, was not so fortunate. A child, who just ten minutes before had been full of life and energy, now lay broken and dead on a Glasgow pavement.

Police and ambulances were on the scene within minutes. As they led Jean Waddell away, her head covered in a coat, the crowd of parents and locals pressed forward angrily and officers had to hold them back.

The unhinged woman had formulated her terrible plan on her way home. She had decided to commit an act so outrageous, so awful that the authorities would be forced to execute her. So she had gathered together seven local children on the pretext of showing them some puppies in her house. Once there, she systematically threw five of them from the front window. The other two escaped when George Sutherland smashed down her door.

But Jean Waddell did not hang. She did not even stand trial, having been found insane and unfit to plead. At her court appearance, which lasted only twenty-five minutes, doctors described her as a chronic paranoid schizophrenic. They said she often imagined herself to be the Empress of Japan. They said she had shown no remorse for what she had done. They said she was more interested in what men thought of her. She sat impassively as the judge ordered her to be detained under Her Majesty's Pleasure in a secure mental institution.

As Jean Waddell began her new life in Carstairs Hospital, Gorbals MP Alice Cullen was asking questions over why Jean Waddell had ever been allowed out in the first place. Doctors, however, countered that she had responded well to treatment and they had no power to keep her locked away.

However, such concern came too late for the little ones. One young life had been snuffed out and six others blighted by injury and trauma. Jean Waddell may have been a victim of her own mental condition but those children were victims too. They and their families had to accept the judgement of the courts but that did not mean they had to forgive. And they could never forget.

13

'TIL DEATH...

Sheila Garvie, 1968

The sixties – they say if you can remember them, you weren't there.

It was a time when the old ways were being torn down. The old morality was being undermined and people were turning on, tuning in and dropping out. Sex was no longer a taboo subject and free love was becoming more of a practice than a concept.

Sex wasn't invented in the Sixties, of course – it merely came out into the open. But, although the decade's changing mood swung freely among some of the young and certain sections of the old, it did not quite reach every level of society. Stories of sexual experimentation could still shock so tabloid newspapers used them both to increase sales and to titillate the pursed-lip brigade who deplored the breakdown of moral values while salivating over the salacious gossip. In Scotland, the case that exemplified the growing permissiveness of the age – and the public's fascination with it – was the Garvie murder.

Wealthy farmer Maxwell Garvie wanted to be a soldier in the sexual revolution. This led him to experiment with drugs and indulge in practices that some might find distasteful. The problem was he wanted his wife to participate and so he propelled her into an affair with a younger man. However, rather than open a new sexual world for him, it forced open a Pandora's box of emotions and everyone found, to their cost, that those who play with sexual fire often get burned.

Sheila Watson fell head over heels for Maxwell Garvie in the mid fifties. They seemed a perfect couple: he was handsome, she was beautiful; he was worth a bob or two, she had spent her life viewing the lifestyles of the rich and famous from the sidelines. As a child, she had lived on the royal estate at Balmoral where her father was a stonemason. On leaving school, she first worked in the local telephone exchange but soon found herself a job at the castle as a maid.

By 1954, her family was living in Stonehaven, south of Aberdeen, and she took a job with a local bus company. It was while attending a dance in the town hall that she first met Maxwell Garvie. Love, as they say, blossomed and, in June 1955, the twenty-one-year-old farmer married his eighteen-year-old bride and the young couple took up residence in Garvie's farm at West Cairnbeg, Fordoun.

Over the following eight years, Sheila gave birth to three children – two girls and a boy. Life for the Garvies could not have been better. But Maxwell thought it could be. By 1962, he was showing an interest in nudism and taking his attractive wife to naturist camps in Britain and abroad. He bought land near Alford in Aberdeenshire and set up his own private club, planting 1000 trees to help shield the naked flesh from the prying eyes of the less liberated. But still this was not enough. He was looking for something more exciting so turned to pornography.

'He seemed to get sex all out of proportion,' said Sheila Garvie at her trial. 'He sent to London for literature and books and pornographic pictures. He just seemed to change.'

Soon he was taking nude pictures of Sheila – and showing them to other men. On first being introduced to one of her husband's acquaintances, the man remarked to Sheila, 'I've seen more of you than you think.'

Showing off naked pictures of his wife was distasteful but harmless compared to Garvie's next move. For he was about to heighten the emotional mix by forcing his wife, already depressed from his apparent personality change, into the arms of a younger man.

Max Garvie first met twenty-one-year-old Brian Tevendale when the young man worked as barman. They were both members of the Scottish National Party and the two seemed to hit it off although Tevendale later claimed that Garvie had more than mere friendship in mind. Soon Tevendale was spending nights at the Garvie farm, often being left alone with his friend's attractive wife. Although nothing untoward seemed to happen at this time, Garvie would ask Sheila what they had got up to while he was away. He wanted to know if they had had sex. The questions he asked were 'absolutely revolting', she said.

Then, one drunken night in September 1967, Garvie pushed his wife into Tevendale's bedroom and left her there. The alcohol reduced their inhibitions and increased their libido, allowing their obvious attraction to become physical for the first time. Later, Garvie questioned Sheila over what had taken place between her and his young friend. Then he demanded that she have sex with him as well.

'It appeared it excited him that I had been with Brian,' she said. 'He got a kick out of it.'

As the relationship between Sheila and Brian grew, Max was embarking on his own extramarital adventures. He had been introduced to Brian's sister, Trudi, who was married to Fred Birse, a policeman in Aberdeen. The two were soon enjoying an affair that often included trips away with Brian and Sheila. Sometimes on these trips, Trudi Birse would be sent to fetch Sheila so that Max could have sex with her as well. Mrs Birse was also instructed to question Brian on his sex life with Sheila and pass on the details to Max. On occasions when Trudi could not attend the weekend sex flings, Max Garvie flipped a coin with Tevendale to see who would sleep with Sheila. After losing twice in a row, Garvie apparently decided that a threesome was the best idea. According to Tevendale, the older man had already expressed an interest in a homosexual liaison with him but Tevendale said he had rebuffed his sexual advances.

But matters were becoming complicated. Physical pleasure was all very well – no one was getting hurt although it was having dreadful effects on their emotional wellbeing. Sheila had fallen in love with Tevendale and vice versa. And it seems that, as far as Max was concerned, the vice was fine but he was none too pleased with the versa.

He stopped seeing Trudi and demanded that Sheila do the same with Brian. At the trial, the court heard he once twisted her arm painfully behind her back, forced her to her knees and held a broken glass to her face in an attempt to make her say, 'Tevendale's a bastard.' She refused and he threw her against a wall. Drink and drugs made him do it, he said later, but, when Sheila left him, he threatened to shoot Tevendale and their children if she did not return. Tevendale, meanwhile, was beaten up twice. During one of the attacks he was cut on the face and he claimed the attacker told him it was a gift from 'the Skipper' – the nickname Tevendale used for Garvie while they were flying the farmer's private plane.

It was clear matters could not continue in this way. Three people were desperately unhappy with their lives. Max Garvie's pursuit of sexual thrills had raised the spectre of losing his wife to another man. Despite his claims that he drew more pleasure from a fortnight with Trudi than he had had in an entire marriage to Sheila, he clearly did not want his wife to leave him.

But, by this time, the Pandora's box of sexual tension had been thrown wide open. It would take blood to close it again.

Maxwell Garvie vanished on 15 May 1968. Curiously, it was his sister who reported him missing. On being questioned, Sheila said that she had woken up that morning to find his side of the bed empty and that she had no idea where he had gone. His blue Cortina was found abandoned on the runway of Fordoun Flying Club, of which he was a founding member, and a massive search began but no trace of the man was found – although it was suggested that he had run away to the continent with another woman. A notice in the Scottish police *Gazette*, with information provided by his wife and Brian Tevendale, stated that Garvie was a free spender, was fond of female company but had strong homosexual tendencies because he was often seen in the company of young men. It also said that he took pep pills and tranquillisers, often with strong drink, and it went on to say that, of late, he had been impulsive, perhaps because of his 'addiction to drink'.

'He has threatened suicide on at least one occasion,' it read. 'Deals in pornographic material and is an active member of nudist camps and an enthusiastic flyer. May have gone abroad.'

For three months there was no sign of him. A file was kept open but Garvie was a grown man and, with no obvious evidence of foul play, there was little for police to go on.

Then, on 16 August, Edith Watson, Sheila's mother, broke the news to police that her son-in-law was dead. Sheila had told her some weeks previously although the word 'murder' was never used. As far as Mrs Watson knew, the death was either self-inflicted or accidental. She did not know exactly what had happened but her daughter had spoken about tides and the elderly woman had the impression that the body had been disposed of at sea. But, when Sheila floated the idea of taking the children away to live with Brian Tevendale, Mrs Watson had to speak out. Max had once asked her to look after the children's interests if anything happened to him – and, above all, to keep them away from Tevendale. As she had never liked the young man anyway, she had agreed.

So, she approached the police, told them what she knew and officers arrested Sheila, Brian and a twenty-one-year-old local man, Andrew Paul – as this person was subsequently cleared, his name has been changed here – for the murder. On 17 August, Tevendale led them to an underground culvert leading from Laurieston Castle near to the village of St Cyrus, where he had been born. There they found Max Garvie's badly beaten corpse, with a bullet wound to the head.

According to Tevendale, the man's death had been an accident. He claimed that a distraught Sheila had phoned him in the middle of the night on 14 May. She and Max had been arguing – as usual, over sex. Tevendale claimed that Sheila was refusing to give into her husband this time and that he had taken up a rifle.

'He said that, if she didn't let him put it up her arse, he'd shoot her,' Tevendale told police. During the subsequent struggle for possession of the rifle, it had gone off, killing Garvie.

Tevendale agreed to help hide the body, taking it to the culvert where he had played as child. After this, he believed he would only be involved as a witness.

But that was not to be, for Andrew Paul – the young man who had unwittingly become involved in the high-stakes game of love and death – told a different story. He said that he and Tevendale had gone to the West Cairnbeg farm to see Max Garvie and had been met by Mrs Garvie, who gave them a drink then took them into an empty room. Tevendale, said the young man, had lifted a rifle from the wall and loaded it with shells from his pocket. About three-quarters of an hour later, Mrs Garvie had come back and told them, 'He's asleep.' She then led them into a bedroom where Paul saw a man lying face down on the bed. Tevendale battered the man over the head with the butt of the rifle before throwing a pillow over the bloody face and firing once. The body was dragged to Paul's Ford Zephyr and Tevendale guided him to the culvert after first leaving Garvie's Cortina at the flying club.

But Trudi Birse said her brother had told her a different story the day after Garvie's death. She had found Brian sitting at the kitchen table, obviously distressed, and she said he had eventually admitted that Paul had beaten Garvie with an iron bar. Tevendale, believing the man to be dead, had shot him in the head. They had then disposed of the body.

Sheila Garvie gave yet another version of that night's events. Yes, she and her husband had argued over sex but they did actually make love and then fell asleep. She said something pulling at her arm had awoken her and that she had found Tevendale standing over the bed. He took her into the bathroom and told her to wait there. At this point she saw there was another man with him. She had taken a sleeping pill, she explained, and was so groggy that she had just done as she was told without questioning it and she had then locked herself in. Next, she had heard a series of terrible thumping sounds coming from the bedroom, followed by a terrible silence. Tevendale then told her to come out and hold the door to the children's bedroom closed. Still doped up, she had continued to do as she was told while he and the other man began to drag a heavy object wrapped in a sheet down the stairs.

Four different versions of one dreadful act – it was Akira Kurosawa's 1950 film, *Rashômon*, with a Scottish accent. There were three people on the first murder charge that Stonehaven Sheriff Court had seen for seventy years. One life had been lost and others were about to be ruined in a story of sex and drugs, jealousy and perversion, love and death.

Observers were expecting a sensational trial. They were not to be disappointed.

It was being called the trial of the decade. Demand for seats in the public gallery of Aberdeen's High Court was so high that queues began to form early on the morning of the first day. The crush of people grew so large that police had to erect crash barriers. In the end, only 100 people could be packed into the space and at least double that turned away.

All three accused pleaded not guilty to the charges, with Sheila Garvie and Andrew Paul each lodging a special defence of impeachment. Garvie claimed the murder was committed by Tevendale or Paul or both and Paul said it was Tevendale or Garvie or both.

The drama began early in the trial when Mrs Watson, Sheila's mother, took the stand and collapsed soon after swearing the oath. The fifty-nine-year-old woman had to be helped away while her daughter watched and wept openly. However, the woman was back the following day and sipped constantly from a glass of water as she recounted all she knew about her daughter's marriage, about the sexual adventuring, about the drug-taking and, finally, why she felt forced to contact the police.

Trudi Birse, Tevendale's sister and the deceased's mistress, spoke about her sexual relationship with Max Garvie, including the foursome trips away. She told the court about her conversation with her brother on the day after the murder. Amazingly, she also admitted helping Sheila Garvie wash Tevendale's bloodstained clothes – and helping her burn sheets from the bed in which Max Garvie was shot. Her policeman husband, Fred, helped dispose of the bloody sheets and burn the mattress – and admitted instructing Sheila how to use an oily rag to wipe fingerprints from a rifle. The couple's involvement in the case would bring them further trouble at the end of the trial.

The skull of the deceased was one of the prosecution exhibits. Two female jurors and Sheila Garvie all looked away as it was produced from a cardboard box for a police officer to examine. Later, when Dr Douglas McBain, a forensic scientist from Aberdeen University, used it to illustrate his evidence, Sheila Garvie took ill and the judge, Lord Thomson, halted the evidence for a five-minute recess.

The Garvies' cleaner explained how the bedroom furniture had been rearranged after her employer's disappearance and that she had been instructed not to clean up. Police later found traces of blood in the room, while the mattress on the bed was obviously far too narrow for the frame. The original, of course, had been burned.

A local minister recalled some gossip about Max Garvie getting a friend to seduce his wife. He also spoke of conversations he had had with Mrs Garvie during one of the couple's separations. In the course of these conversations, she told him of her husband's 'perverted' sexual demands and she had claimed that he had had homosexual leanings. The minister said that he found this 'difficult to attribute to the man [he] knew' but a book, entitled *Sexual Techniques of the Human Female* ,was produced. This allegedly belonged to the dead man and a page, detailing how a husband could encourage his wife to have affairs, was turned down with paragraphs highlighted.

Andrew Paul insisted he had no idea what was going to happen that night. He had kept his silence about the bloody acts, he claimed, because he feared Tevendale would kill him too. Tevendale had even acted as his best man during his July wedding and Sheila

Garvie had been a maid of honour. A police officer, who knew both men, said that the young man was easily led and that Tevendale was, in his opinion, a very dominating character.

For her part, Sheila Garvie blamed herself for the murderous events although she insisted she was not present when the deed was done. Tevendale did what he did to protect her, she said, and afterwards she protected him because she loved him.

'I felt morally responsible for what happened that night,' she said. 'I had got Brian involved so deeply that I felt I unconsciously provoked him into an emotional state and he had acted upon it.'

During her nine hours in the witness box, former Sunday School teacher Sheila Garvie told the court how she had contemplated suicide during the three months between the killing and her arrest.

'I did not know how long I could live with the secret,' she said.

However, the prosecution tried to paint her as a Lady Macbeth who had plotted the murder and had led her lover into the actual act. There could have been no late-night phone call to Tevendale, it was insisted, because there was no record of it at the exchange. And there was no burning or powder mark around the bullet wound so Tevendale's claims, that he had stood over the bed and fired, could be discounted.

Sheila Garvie's QC said that the case was like 'Lady Chatterley with a tragic ending'. He said that Maxwell Garvie had created 'not only a permissive society within his own home, not only a foursome group, which he thought was in the best traditions of a modern enlightened society, but was creating a Frankenstein's monster that eventually rose up and slew him.'

The idea, of course, was to convince the jury that Mrs Garvie had been forced into involvement in the murder by circumstances and her husband's debasing sexual appetites. However, the judge reminded the jury that this was not a court of morality. The court had heard much about Maxwell Garvie's sexual predilections but, he said, 'it is just as much murder in our law to kill such a man as it is to kill a man who is sexually normal and whose morals are beyond reproach.'

The jury, reduced to nine men and five women after the illness of a sixth female member, took just under an hour to reach their verdict. The charge against Andrew Paul was found not proven but both Sheila Garvie and Brian Tevendale were sentenced to life.

A shaken Sheila Garvie was led from the court although one press report claimed that, as she passed Tevendale's mother, she whispered, 'I want to marry Brian.' Reporters also stated the two were reunited for one final time in the cells below for a tearful farewell but Sheila Garvie herself has denied this. Tevendale did, however, write to her later saying he had asked the Secretary of State for Scotland for permission to marry her. All she needed to do was write to the Crown Office and make the same request but she decided against it.

Fred and Trudi Birse had their own ordeal to go through. On leaving court after the sentences were heard, they were surrounded by an angry 2000-strong mob chanting, 'Hang them – lynch them . . .' Clearly, the public was unhappy with the Birses' part in the case that had captured so many imaginations. The couple managed to take shelter in the nearby offices of a national newspaper until the police could spirit them away in a taxi.

Sheila Garvie began her sentence in Greenock's Gartside Prison. Six months after her arrival, she learned that her mother had died but was refused permission to attend the funeral in Stonehaven. In 1975, she became the first registered inmate at the brand new Corton Vale Prison in Stirlingshire. Three years later she was released to begin a new life although subsequent marriages proved unsuccessful. She has never spoken about the events of 1968 but, in 1980, she published a book telling her side of the story.

As far as is known, she has not seen Brian Tevendale since that final day in court. Whatever drove the unhappy couple – whether it was love or lust – was not strong enough to bring them together again.

Bibliography

Adams, Norman (1996), *Scotland's Chronicles of Blood* (Robert Hale, London)

Bailey, Brian (1989), *Hangmen of England* (W H Allen, London)

— (2002) *Burke and Hare: The Year of the Ghouls* (Mainstream, Edinburgh)

Barnett, Ratcliffe (1952), *Border By-ways and Lothian Lore* (John Grant, Edinburgh)

Bell, J J (1932), *The Glory of Scotland* (Harrap, London)

Brown, Michael (1994), *James I* (Canongate, Edinburgh)

Cheetham, J Keith (1999), *On the Trail of Mary, Queen of Scots* (Luath Press, Edinburgh)

Chesney, Kellow (1970), *The Victorian Underworld* (Maurice Temple Smith, London)

Donaldson, Gordon (1992), *Scottish Kings* (Barnes & Noble, London)

Earle, Peter (1972), *The Life and Times of Henry V* (Weidenfeld and Nicolson)

Fido, Martin (1988), *Bodysnatchers: A History of the Resurrectionists* (Weidenfeld and Nicolson, London)

Forbes, George and Meehan, Paddy (1982), *Such Bad Company* (Paul Harris, Edinburgh)

Gaute, J H H and Odell, Robin (1979), *Murderers' Who's Who* (Harrap, London)

— (1982), *Murder Whatdunit* (Harrap, London)

Garvie, Sheila (1980), *Married to Murder* (Chambers, Edinburgh)

Grant, James (1982), *Old and New Edinburgh* (Lang Syne Publishers, Glasgow)

Horan, Martin (1990), *Scottish Executions, Assassinations and Murders* (Chambers, Edinburgh)

Huson, Richard (ed.), *Sixty Famous Trials* (*Daily Express*, London)

Knox, Bill (1968), *Court of Murder* (John Long, London)

Bibliography

Lane, Brian (1991), *The Murder Guide* (BCA, London)

— (1992), *The Encylopedia of Forensic Science* (Headline, London)

Livingstone, Sheila (2000), *Confess and Be Hanged* (Birlinn, Edinburgh)

Love, Dane (1989), *Scottish Kirkyards* (Robert Hale, London)

MacClure, Victor, *She Stands Accused* (J B Lippincott, Philadelphia)

MacGregor, Forbes (1983), *More MacGregor's Mixture* (Gordon Wright, Edinburgh)

MacLean, Fitzroy (1995), *Highlanders* (David Campbell, London)

Morton, H V (1929), *In Search of Scotland* (Methuen, London)

— (1933), *In Scotland Again* (Methuen, London)

Mure MacKenzie, Agnes (1935), *Rise of the Stewarts* (Alexander MacLehose, Edinburgh)

Prebble, John (1971), *The Lion in the North* (Secker & Warburg, London)

Roughead, William (1995), *Twelve Scots Trials* (Mercat Press, Edinburgh)

Saunders, George (1991), *Casebook of the Bizarre* (John Donald, Edinburgh)

Smith, Sydney (1959), *Mostly Murder* (Harrap, London)

Tod, T M (1938), *The Scots Black Kalendar* (Munro & Scott, Perth)

Whittington-Egon, Molly (1998), *Scottish Murder Stories* (Neil Wilson, Glasgow)

Wilson, Alan J, Brogan, Des and McGrail, Frank (1991), *Ghostly Tales and Sinister Stories of Old Edinburgh* (Mainstream, Edinburgh)

Wilson, Colin and Seaman, Donald (1983), *The Encyclopedia of Modern Murder* (Arthur Barker, London)

Young, Alex F (1998), *Encyclopedia of Scottish Executions 1750–1963* (Eric Dobby, Edinburgh)

Index

190